Freeman's
Change

Est. 2015

Edited by

John Freeman

Grove Press UK

First published in the United States of America in 2021 by Grove Atlantic
First published in Great Britain in 2021 by Grove Press UK,
an imprint of Grove Atlantic

Copyright © 2021 by John Freeman

Managing Editor: Julia Berner-Tobin

Copy Editor: Kirsten Giebutowski

All pieces are copyright © 2021 by the author of the piece.
Permission to use any individual piece must be obtained from its author.

"Chick Truck" by Yoko Ogawa was first published in 2006 in
Umi (Tokyo: Shinchosha, pp. 107-135).

"Up Our Sleeves" by Jakuta Alikavazovic was first published in the
September 18, 2020 issue of *Libération*.

1 3 5 7 9 8 6 4 2

A CIP record for this book is available from the British Library.

Grove Press UK
Ormond House
26–27 Boswell Street
London
WC1N 3JZ

www.groveatlantic.com

Trade paperback ISBN 978 1 61185 434 3
Ebook ISBN 978 1 61185 879 2

Printed and bound in Great Britain by Bell & Bain Ltd, Glasgow

Contents

Introduction

JOHN FREEMAN

It's hard to imagine, but the heavens, as we know them, are younger than Shakespeare. They're practically newborn when compared to the practice of mastectomy, which was safely performed as far back as 3500 BC. And they're but a novelty when compared to technology such as the hand-axe, which is half-a-million years old. As late as the early 1500s, the night sky was gazed upon like a ceiling. A gracefully illustrated, but essentially depthless decoration, tilting through our view—comets like brief scars of newness—earth at the center.

It took a mathematician from what is today Poland—Nicolaus Copernicus—a lifetime of study, and one gloriously titled posthumous book (*On the Revolutions of the Celestial Spheres*) to displace earth from the center of the universe. Before he died, Copernicus dedicated his essay to the pope in a move that seems part entreaty, part apology. He knew what he was proposing was nearly blasphemous. It proved to have enormous implications for faith.

It also kicked off a wave of scientific discovery, which Galileo Galilei turned into a full-fledged revolution.

Change can come this way—a door shoved open by a radical idea, truth finally let free. On the back of Copernicus's proofs,

Galileo began to replace an immutable world with one in constant flux. Among his greatest inventions were the instruments to see it change: the reflector telescope, with which he studied the moon; the scientific method, which applied to every known phenomenon; the thermometer; even a version of the compass. In thanks for his efforts, Galileo was tried in 1633 by the Church for heresy and convicted. He spent the rest of his life under house arrest, a period during which he wrote two of his greatest books.

Change is often resisted not simply for what it threatens, but for the new responsibilities it forces upon us. If the universe is a living, dying, and constantly evolving organism, as Galileo suspected, and other astronomers like William Herschel began to surmise in the late eighteenth century, what does this mean about our planet? Can we simply use it with impunity? Meanwhile, on we tilt, observers or passersby, engaged or aloof, meteors through a brief slash of time.

Centuries on from the pre-Copernican era, we can feel somehow made by that old universe; as in, we long for some degree of immutability. For a love which is forever; parents who do not age; the stability of work or occupation. The need to sustain a belief in permanence has created whole religions; art forms; enlightened or regressive political movements. Tents of comfort in the face of what the body knows: we are born into a world of constant change.

From the cells of our body, to the nations we call home, change defines the parameters of life. We are marked by it, and by how and what we resist. We are made by the ways we narrativize our reactions to rupture; how we adapt to what we must accept. Coming in the wake of the worst global pandemic since the ongoing AIDS crisis, this issue of *Freeman's* aims to gather stories, poems, essays, and reports from this shifting front.

*   *   *

We begin with the life of Galileo—not the astronomer, but the newborn son of poet Joshua Bennett. In a brief essay Bennett describes the rituals he and his child—christened August Galileo, after the playwright and the scientist (and a speech of W.E.B. Du Bois's titled after him) begin every morning. They sing to a songbook, they dance to a soundtrack. Why don't we make up new habits? This tends to be the question behind every story or novel Sayaka Murata writes, including her latest story, "Final Days," set in an imagined world of endless life, in which a craze for early death sweeps across Japan.

Sometimes change itself becomes the fantasized ritual. In her powerful memoir, Lina Mounzer recalls the forever delayed, yet constantly imagined improvements her father predicted would transform their lives after they left Lebanon during its civil war. Keeping this hope aloft against the realities of their lives in post-emigration Montreal drives him to the addictive cycles of the lottery. Sulaiman Addonia grew up in a refugee camp in East Africa and learned a similar lesson there about the world's indifference to his attempts to wish it better.

Observing the world's indifference can occasion a search for new metaphors. In Ocean Vuong's exquisite short piece, a man's life is narrated backwards, and with each step into the before time, the inexorability of what just happened lifts away, like smoke. Meantime, after her father dies of Covid, Christy NaMee Eriksen learns she has inadvertently—using the word "avalanche" for how it feels—captured how suddenness is often the accumulation of unbearable pressures.

We have names for such pressures, for stories where such force is euphemized. History is one of them. In her essay on Algeria, Zahia Rahmani reveals how the name of a nation can become a repository for the million unremarked-upon simultaneous changes—and hands—that make a place what it is. Her daring piece, which weaves personal essay, colonial historiography, and twenty-first-century travelogue, suggests one nimble way to tell that story more honestly.

So many people, through no fault of their own, are trapped in tropes they did not elect. This can be infuriating . . . and lethal. Lana Bastašić's vivid short story shows the thin line between these poles as a teenage girl walks home across a city where men pursue her threateningly. In Yoko Ogawa's story, a gentler interpretation of youth and age spins about a man and a child who must step briefly out of their roles to save each other from crushing lonelinesses.

Another arena in which change is formalized are elections. It's a small word for the tumult of chaos, hope, bamboozlement, brave activism, and brutal suppression which fall upon its remit. Elizabeth Ayre's stylish remembrance of the night of November 3rd, 2020, recalls some part of that day's singularity, also the desultoriness which can arise out of the suspicions nothing will change.

Watching the unchangeable in its inexorable march in circles can move one to states of psychosis and rage, grief and communion. Lassitude. The narrator of Kamel Daoud's short story visits all these way stations as his mother begins to die, and regresses to the girl she once was, editing her son from memory in favor of one who left home long ago. In Kyle Dillon Hertz's short memoir, the author winds up in hospital, overtaken by the damage he's done to his own heart with drugs; he finds his communion in the offering of help from a close friend.

* * *

We pass the lamp of hope to hands we trust may keep it safe. Another word for history might be: the story of what happens to that lamp. Several pieces in this issue imagine their way into such handoffs. Aleksandar Hemon's poem about Walter Benjamin appreciates how fantastical was the philosopher's journey in 1940 across the Pyrenees away from Nazis, what force of mind it must have taken to avoid the clutch of despair. Great change, sometimes, can only be faced in the moment. Yasmine El Rashidi's memoir of her family's move from their treasured home upon the Nile reveals how melancholic this passage is when it has been a long time coming.

Adaptation to great change does not always mean acceptance. It can coexist with modes of resistance, with equivocal feeling, with regret. These are all part of Adania Shibli's luminescent tale of a man building a small business of bus lines in contemporary Palestine. The acrobatics of his adjustment to the daily disruptions of life under occupation are seen in sharp contrast to the steady grind of building a business.

Change can lag behind its necessity by decades, centuries even, out of which develop strategies of deflection. Rickey Laurentiis's intricately beautiful poem enacts the way their gender flummoxes its so called viewers, turning the poem's speaker into a one-person help desk of explanation. Style, in this ecstatic mode, is beyond fashion, a crucial buffer. In her bracing memoir, Lauren Groff explores how going back to her hometown is impossible, for it would render her that too exposed, too seen, too vulnerable child she once was—so each night she sacrifices this child to the lake in her mind.

Great change often makes martyrs of people who simply can deflect no longer. For the past year, poet and translator Valzhyna Mort has read the news from her home country of Belarus in search of names of the dead. Here she translates poets who have found themselves unable to turn away from their government's tyranny any longer, on the front lines of political change. Their words are burning embers of a not-yet-made historical moment.

Some of the most imagistic writing here reveals the human figure amidst great flux. We need this in art and poetry to understand where we are and what is happening. In her poem, stark as a black-and-white photograph, Sandra Cisneros captures the face of a boy sitting in the back of a truck, a machine gun in his lap. A soldier in Mexico's sprawling narco-violence. Julia Alvarez's brilliant poem neatly inverts the framework of background and foreground, the poet remembering herself in the 1970s: a recent graduate living in Queens who would, along the course of a subway journey that took her into Manhattan to work at a department store, transform herself into a very different woman.

There are no do-overs, no backstops to certain types of change. We may create games, as Jakuta Alikavazovic writes in her short essay, to allow ourselves the fantasy that we can go back to the way things were before. But these games cannot be played forever. Alejandro Zambra spent years fantasizing about downsizing his library, he writes in his playful, heartfelt memoir, but when he finally does so it is because he has left the family whom he began it with—a fact which gives his new bookshelves a melancholic spareness. In a stilling posthumous poem, Mark Strand shows how the game many of us played growing up—peering out a moving car, bus, or train, listing what one sees—when played as an adult produces very different results. Among them, respect for the blur of time, an awareness of ghosts.

In ancient mythology, change often comes in the form of a monster. A daemon, a spectral presence. Before Galileo, a comet was often viewed as portending sudden catastrophe. Even though we know such things to be superstitious, we need to dream our fears to survive change. To push them outside ourselves in forms of art, narration, design. In Lina Meruane's incredible gothic story, a woman trapped inside a house with her two sons during a pandemic faces the barbarity of the ultimate sacrifice demanded of her as a mother. Meanwhile, in Cristina Rivera Garza's astonishing rewriting of the myth of a mermaid, we watch a man blown sideways by a woman not his wife. Only this time they're on a mountain, and here the sea is a canopy of green.

We have other recording devices for what has happened beyond our lifetimes, for noting what we've survived, aside from what Galileo, Newton, and others gave us. Not to mention the narrative strategies writer like Jane Austen, Toni Morrison, and Barry Lopez among others pioneered as ways to remember history. A forest, after all, is a living record of change. In the carbon content of plant life and the patterning of tree rings lurks a nearly complete story of the past, if we can only listen. In a dispatch from the forests of Montana, where human intervention has begun to deform the landscape's own ability to heal and recover, Rick Bass delivers a stirring call to pay attention to the reverberations which travel through wood. Some of you, perhaps, reading this right now, sit upon a piece of it. Maybe, if this is a paper copy of *Freeman's*, you are reading from it. Later tonight, maybe an even smaller number of you will gaze out the window through it. Galileo's original telescope was made of two pieces of wood, joined together, to form a tube. And so he saw the heavens from earth. What stories it tells, what dramas it contains—like the stars assembled here.

Freeman's

Change

Seven Shorts

GIANT STEPS

There is a playlist on my phone that's built entirely from the genius of John Coltrane, and I've been playing it for my son since the day he was born. It begins with Trane's cover of "My Favorite Things." In truth, I have no idea how it ends, because we never get there. By the time we arrive at "Lush Life" or "Equinox" during the azure hours of the early morning, he's usually asleep again, or else we have decided that we're done dancing across the kitchen and are onto another activity. We have a few hours before Mom wakes up. The options unfold like a field before us. Most days, we move right from the dances to time with poems, as that feels like the most logical sequence. Early mornings, after all, are made for music.

Some recent favorites—and you should know that my sense of the work's reception is based on feedback in the form of ear-to-ear smiles, and yelling in the midst of one or more stanzas in direct succession—include Joy Priest's "Little Lamp," Al Young's "The Mountains of California: Part I," and "Something New Under the Sun" by Steve Scafidi. The Scafidi poem opens with the sentence *It would have to shine,* and every one of the days that begins this way seems to. Even deep gray weather takes on new resonance:

hours to spend watching sheets of rain re-arrange the backyard, making it much too muddy for our family dog, Apollo V, to play in. He doesn't always take this sort of shift in his routine well, Apollo, as he has recently had to adjust to having a new family member, and is still getting used to the feeling that not all of our attention is focused on him.

This conundrum is mostly my fault. And in more ways than one, perhaps, naming him as I did for a god of poetry and light, a space shuttle, the theater where my mother first saw Smokey Robinson sing, and a cinematic revision of the greatest boxer of all time, his modern legacy renewed in the body of Michael B. Jordan. I'm named after a book in the Bible and an older brother who died before I was born. My mother takes her first name from her grandmother, and her second from the tall, Puerto Rican nurse in the delivery room where my grandmother first guided her into the world.

My son, August Galileo, has a name that emerges from both African diaspora literature and a family commitment to studying the heavens. He is named for the legendary poet and playwright, August Wilson, as well as for Black August: the yearly commemorative event in which people all across the world celebrate not only the revolutionary legacy of George Jackson, who was slain on August 21, 1971, but also the practice of freedom across a much larger stretch of human history; the founding of the Underground Railroad, the Nat Turner Rebellion, and the Haitian Revolution. *Galileo* is meant to gesture both toward the father of modern astronomy, and the 1908 Fisk University speech delivered by W.E.B. Du Bois that bears his name: "Galileo Galilei." It is one of the most powerful pieces of oratory I have ever encountered. In it, Du Bois writes: "And you, graduates of Fisk University, are the watchmen on the outer wall. And you, Fisk University, Intangible but real Personality, builded of Song and Sorrow, and the Spirits of Just Men made perfect, are as one standing Galileo—wise before the Vision of Death and the Bribe of the Lie."

Names are an incantation of a certain kind. *August Galileo* reminds us, and will hopefully remind our son, to have courage in the face of unthinkable odds. Persistence in the midst of the seemingly impossible. An unflinching dedication to wonder, respect for the essential drama of human life, and the ceremonies that make it worthwhile.

The other big difference since August's arrival—aside from the new routine at sunrise—is that there are toys everywhere. Many of which have names that are not to be found on the boxes we purchased them in: the Wolf Throne (his swing), the Device (a gray baby sling), and the Rattle Snail (a rattle shaped just like a snail). This ever-expanding collective of objects makes it hard to walk through the living room, but a joy to be there. Once Mom comes downstairs, it's party time once again. We throw on a KAYTRANADA deejay set and dance until we are tired, falling to the couch in unison, where we rest for a while.

One of the great gifts of the Black expressive tradition is that it refuses the notion of human immortality—especially as it is often imagined in our secular modernity, through private property or conquest—and yet gives you moments where you feel invincible, endless. We do not live forever. But we do live on. We live for the children. We engage in protracted struggle so that they might inherit a planet worthy of their loveliness. While I once understood this largely in the abstract, this sense of things now animates my days. I can't hear Coltrane without thinking of my boy arriving here just a few months ago on a Sunday night, hours before dawn. Two weeks ago, while looking through old records, I found a copy of Trane's debut with Atlantic, *Giant*

Steps. It felt like a sign. New beginnings, infinite promise. The intractable power of a single human breath, enough to shift the known world on its axis.

—Joshua Bennett

DEEP PERSISTENT SLAB

Previously I only used the word avalanche as a verb. It basically meant, "I am crying and I cannot stop."

Still, owning a home in an avalanche zone, I have recently been compelled to try to make sense of my city's urban avalanche advisories. They use the word avalanche in a way that means "a massive amount of snow, ice, and rocks falling down a mountainside."

Please forgive my errors or oversimplification, but here's my attempt at translating. It appears that it matters what kind of day a mountain is having. Depending on the weather, snow settles into different kinds of layers, and these layers stack up over time. What I understand to be our biggest current problem is what's called a "deep persistent slab."

A deep persistent slab is a big piece of snow with a very weak layer inside it. The weak layer is so deep you almost don't know it's there unless you're looking for it. Another layer inside it might be a crust, which in a way amplifies the weak layer because you could poke the crust a long ways away and the poke would reverberate across the crust, and this is how one light touch could trigger an avalanche of giant proportions. No matter how soft or how strong the snow is, if you touch it when or where it is tender, it will drop to the depth and the width of its weakest part. And so an avalanche is not just snow, and it is not just the trigger, it is the result of holding too much when you were not properly grounded.

On the same day, one year apart, I packed a bag. That's a lie; one year ago my friend Melissa packed my bag, because I was avalanching on the living room floor. My sister had called. My father was fighting for his life in the ICU. At that time they said they didn't think he would make it through the night, and I could not fly out until morning.

Sometimes you don't get a warning

I can't separate the experience of saying goodbye to the home my dad built me from the experience of saying goodbye to my dad at this precise time last year. There are all kinds of natural disasters. They say our bodies remember grief anniversaries, which baffles me since my own grief is very bad at time management. Perhaps grief is just a weak layer and it doesn't matter how deep it's buried. A smell or a bird or the sunrise on a particular day can always touch it.

Grief, I mean the director of emergency management, knocked on my door Saturday morning to explain the danger of wishing for the best.

But it's a blessing, isn't it, to have a chance. To have a minute. To take the irreplaceable with you.

If the avalanche were to hit our homes, they predicted it could be fourteen feet deep going fifty-seven mph across a quarter mile. I really can't see how a human house could survive that, and yet I am familiar with praying against the odds. My father survived his first night, and on the second night, he briefly woke up. It was today, one year ago: my mother's birthday. A miracle, they said, and the nurses had chills. It filled me with catastrophic hope.

When we dug our way out, we told my dad that we loved him, and that he didn't have to worry about us. This was the third day. We said goodbye, because we were warned; and it's better to say goodbye and walk away than to be destroyed inside it. That was 364 days ago. Some mornings I can walk on that layer and some mornings I'm still buried under the snow.

What type of weather do we want? my friends asked, and I don't know enough avalanche science beyond "we want spring" to answer this. In grief counseling, no weather is bad; I think the goal is that you heal your deep persistent layers so no slab could kill you. The director of emergency management lowered the danger level from "extreme" to "high," so I know that with the right conditions even an avalanche can change. The weak layer can strengthen, the facets can face the wind. The load can lighten and aspects can melt. It can be touched without breaking.

Often it just takes time

—Christy NaMee Eriksen

LAKE

Some nights, that deep cold lake brings my child self back to me again. This is often without my consent. I want no part of the person I was then, or to be back in the town of those years that made and held me. Cooperstown, where I was born, is a speck in-the-middle-of-nowhere New York, so small it is officially a hamlet, so pretty with its flower boxes and groomed hedges and American flags that it has been transformed into an object, its citizens offering the place up every summer for the pleasure of thousands of boys and men who come for baseball and nostalgia and a glimpse of their own child-ghosts. Can a town be objectified like a woman? If she is Cooperstown, she can.

In my dreams, the lake first sets me down at the Presbyterian church atop Pioneer Street, thin, tall, ancient, a building made of whittled bones, where I was long ago given the gift of awe but also of torment, the three-hour services with an indifferently talented choir and the crotch of my itchy woolen tights slowly sliding down my thighs. Through the rest of the week, I would bear the oppressive weight of a male god who was always furious at the tiny rebellions of my mind. I was defective because I feared far more than I loved. A mouse, this child me, blonde, pale, blinking, bewildered, scared. In the dreams, even as I repudiate her, this child self goes away from the church as fast as she can, flying down the hill toward Main Street. It is empty of cars and people, the single stoplight westward along the street shining against the wet asphalt, glazing the windows of the bakery in alternate red and gold and green, the cord of the great flagpole in the center of the street where I stand chiming in the small wind. From there, the street scoops downhill to Lakefront Park, where the statue of Natty Bumppo hunts with his dog, until at last it empties out into the dark glower of the lake.

It is this strange long lake, a block away, that peered from over the lawn into the windows of my childhood bedroom. Before I rose from bed every morning I would look out to gauge the lake's mood that day, which could change with terrifying swiftness. There would be temper tantrums when the dust-devils grabbed loose snow up from the ice and spun it to frantic dancing; placid happy days of sunlight on the warm, navy blue August water; pensive sheets of fog lifting gently off its surface in an orange autumn dawn; thunderstorms descending from Cherry Valley nine miles north in luxurious woolen sheets of gray. We had a party every

Fourth of July, where from our lawn we'd watch the fireworks double themselves on the water below, the hills grabbing the thunder of the explosions and tossing it back and forth between them until a new blast came and the old thunder was lost. The lake has always been pure intensity, beauty, terror to me.

And in my dreams the child me stands hapless at the flagpole, trying to resist its pull, but inevitably the lake draws my ghost down, toward this wild and uncontrollable and inescapable depth of feeling.

This is what I dislike, the way that as a child I felt absolutely everything, and it was all unbearable. I had a good childhood, I was fed and loved, but I was born unskinned, a girl bleeding out her hot red emotion everywhere. There were days I felt I would die of the sound of the crows eating the corn in my father's garden or the taste of the honey I stole from the back of the pantry—sugar forbidden in my house, pleasure suspect—and spread surreptitiously on the hot biscuits I baked before swim practice. The membrane between my interior self and the world was easily rent. I could contain nothing within me. I am not quite sure how I survived. And everywhere I went in town, even in places where you couldn't see the lake, you knew it was there, gleaming; it was my overlarge mirror, unskinned like me, shining the sky back to itself, too emotional, too much, too dangerous, you could drown in it.

A dreamer at last awakens into life. The lake's nighttime draw fades until I wake in the mornings as an adult who has grown the calluses necessary to keep herself alive. Still, even as an adult, I am reluctant to come home. It has been almost a decade since I've been back to Cooperstown; my parents have moved away, there is no obvious reason to return. And so I have kept the place safe, stuck in aspic, somewhere deep inside. There is a beauty in this resistance, because the layers of time and space in me can be preserved unmixed. In this way, the bend where Lake Street descends to Council Rock exists as many things all at once: the spot where one Halloween in middle school, I lay down in the dark road to scare myself and was nearly run over by some quiet car, where I stepped on a flotsam board and drove a nail through my foot, where my first friend and I crouched, seven years old, scraping wet stones on stones to paint our faces and make ourselves warriors. To see the ways the town has changed, the trees loved decades ago dead and vanished, the buildings altered, the old friends startlingly old and stout and gray, looking like their parents as they bend their heads into the wind, crossing the street, no, no thank you, I cannot, it would be too much. The fragile defenses I have constructed against the overwhelm of the world would break. Anyone could see straight into my depths. And so I sacrifice, night after night, my child self to the lake, both self and lake through dream rendered subject, not object. Perhaps a ghost is a person and a place dreaming at the same time. I let my subconscious draw this trembling, world-sick child down to Lakefront Park, which in my sleep is simultaneously draped in night and too brightly daylit, the sun blazing the water hurts my eyes. In this place I once saw a flock of mallards peck a sickly drake to death, and my golden retriever would hie herself there to lap up the grease the motel's restaurant set outside to cool, and my lovelorn best friend and I would eat whole pints of ice cream to find a foothold for self-hatred, and I once waded in after a frisbee and sank up to my hips in duck shit and had to be pulled out with a rope. All of it, all, remains as it has ever been, living, tender, wild.

—Lauren Groff

THE POWER OF ABSENCE:
CHILDHOOD BUSINESS VENTURES IN A REFUGEE CAMP

The mother of my childhood friend was a sex worker. I remember how, when I encountered them outside our school in the mornings, he'd hug her tightly as if he wanted to collect the fragments she had broken into under the weight of clients during the night, piecing her together again between his arms.

Many parents in our camp were only complete and present in the mirrors of our imaginations. My own mother was away, working in Saudi Arabia as a domestic servant for a princess, and had left me and my siblings under the care of my maternal grandmother when I was about three. But like my friend, I too embraced my mother every morning, even with the Red Sea between us. I embraced her in the old memories she left behind, and the new ones that wafted into my world from the cassette tapes she sent us from Jeddah along with the framed color photo which my grandmother had hung on the mud wall of our hut.

Admittedly, though, I had contradictory feelings about my mother. I missed her but her absence destabilised my childhood as adults reminded me of the reasons for her departure almost every day. I would be told about her immeasurable sacrifices—that she left so she could earn money to take us out of the camp alive—whenever I misbehaved, when I wouldn't do something asked of me, like going to fetch water with our donkey from the river hours away, or not doing my homework on time.

Children, I would discover, also pay prices for their parents' sacrifices. Only these are not often noticed by adults, because they take place under the child's skin. The loss of my mother was like an underpainting of a canvas that would be the foundation of my childhood.

I became too polite, too grateful to the people who looked after me, going out of my way to please them, trying to alleviate in whatever way I could the burden of being a parentless child on their shoulders. I would be careful not to do anything that would tarnish my mother's reputation. I turned myself into a shell of what I knew I was. The child that roamed the camp was a made-up one, the real one was buried inside me under piles of a mother's absence and its consequences.

Looking back, I'm convinced it was my desire to fill this gaping hole in my life that led me to embark on a series of small business ideas when I was eight or nine.

The first of those was to sell sweets and cigarettes. I remember the morning I sat on the bed I shared with my brother in our hut, looking up at the framed color photo of my mother hanging on the wall. With her hair braided, and wearing a traditional zuria dress, she looked regal. The way she sat with crossed legs, her hands intertwined around her knees, and her neck long and graceful, reminds me now of Frida Kahlo's self-portrait in a velvet dress, of a woman living in defiance of the pain in her life.

Such was the power of her absence that the wall on which her framed color photo hung was like a black hole, constantly pulling me towards it.

I forced myself to look away from my mother's photo. I counted the savings I had made over the months. The shillings given to me by relatives visiting us from towns and cities now added up to a few Sudanese pound notes. I exited the hut with my money. My grandmother was baking Eritrean bread, in the way she did most mornings. She slammed the dough on the mogogo stove and leaned back from the smoke rising from the stove. I caught her talking to herself. From her I understood that conversing with the self wasn't a sign of insanity, but that sometimes, we are our own, and perhaps only, listeners.

I headed to the market. I chose a shop owned by a relative of my aunt's husband, thinking perhaps he'd be easier to haggle with.

I wanted sweets and cigarettes, I told the light-skinned man in jalabiya and taqiyah. Cigarettes? He wagged his finger at me, saying he was going to have a word with my grandmother, reminding me that my mother was toiling far away in a foreign country for me, and that this was how I was going to repay her? It was a familiar sermon, but like all the sermons I'd heard it gently pressed my true self deeper into the sea of loss inside me. I needed to save myself.

I reassured him that in fact I wanted to start a shop to help my mother by making some money. He patted me on the head and soon after, we talked business. He mentioned a price for a handful of sweets and for each of the single cigarettes. I didn't have enough for a whole pack. I can't remember how many I bought, but I instinctively offered half of what he asked.

Back at home, without informing anyone, I put the sweets in a glass jar and returned to the main street with one of our stools and a small table. I laid out my products. The street was deserted. I didn't have shelter from the afternoon sun, but I had a smile on my face, as if I'd already grasped the mantra that there was no gain without sweat.

When a few eagles flew low past me, I observed the focus in their eyes, that persistent glare for their goal that gave anchor to their wings even when they paused mid air.

Then my first customer approached. He is forever etched in my memory. He was tall and his hair anointed with butter. He wanted a cigarette and asked for the price. I don't know what I said, but it was close to double what I paid for it. He took one and lit it. He was about to leave when he turned and left me his box of matches, saying, you'll need it for your next customers.

But my next customer was Silence whistling towards me on the wings of hot wind. The way to survive was to emulate nature in its sheer intensity and ability to reimagine itself.

My business picked up gradually over the following days and weeks. Between occasional customers, funeral processions, boys and girls scurrying here and there, women saddled with children and others with sadness like jute sacks on their backs, I could see my dream soaring, a reunion with my mother pending, and the life of freedom and self-dependency I had wanted as blazing as the sun hanging between the thatched roofs.

I was perhaps experiencing the elation present in the first lines of Margaret Atwood's poem, "Flying Inside Your Own Body." Deflation would follow soon. One day, my business collapsed. The beginning of decline in my already meager revenue started when a cousin of mine, whose father fled to the camp with his wealth, borrowed money from him and set up a kiosk just meters away from where I was. Unlike me, who had just a stool and a table, he built a thatched kiosk with a veranda.

He sold halva, chewing gum, sesame oil extracted by a cow-powered mill in the market, and some drinks, as well as sweets and cigarettes. The varieties he offered as well as the shade from the sun attracted customers who might otherwise have come my way. But I persisted and invested most of what I earned into buying more sweets than cigarettes. Then one morning it all came to an end when my brother and I had a fight and he took my jar of sweets and smashed it on the muddy ground of our compound.

If a family rivalry combined with a siblings' quarrel led to the end of my first business, the absence of a clinic in the camp made me eat my next.

The camp, one of the two I lived in, had grown over the eight years I was there. It attracted many from nearby towns.

Sudanese as well as Hausa Muslims from Nigeria moved into our camp. The Nigerians became the main owners of pigeon farms, which were increasingly profitable businesses. The birds were bred for the quality of their meat that also contained healing properties.

It was during a morning trip to the river for water that I came across the Nigerian compound full of pigeons. I leaned over the thatched fence where a young girl in front of a hut was pounding grain in a wooden mortar. The pigeons behind her in a large cage cooed loudly. I came back the next day with some of my savings and bought a couple of pigeons and a cage from the Nigerian family. I learned how to feed pigeons, train them, make them feel comfortable, and learned what conditions were needed to make them mate and lay eggs fast.

Our compound was full of wings flapping, pigeons dancing in the air, fighting, coming and going, and the scent of their excrement. Word went around. I sold one or two to begin with. Things were looking up and I planned to buy another bigger cage when I had an accident.

I was playing football with my friends on a hill littered with pebbles when I tripped and fell with my left arm underneath me. It was only when I rose to my feet, and all my friends screamed in shock, that I noticed my hand dangling by my side. I completely dislocated my elbow. I ran home screaming with pain.

The nearest clinic to our camp, the Red Cross, was about a day's drive away, over an unpaved road and then a wooden boat crossing. A male relative tied a scarf around my elbow and demanded that I keep it immobile. Without pain relief, I couldn't sleep. I howled and cried for days. A week or so later, a traditional bonesetter came to see me from across the river. And as he wrapped a wooden splint with cloth around my elbow, I heard him tell my grandmother that he saw pigeons on his way into the hut. "Give him pigeon soup for the next few weeks," he said. "This is the best meat to strengthen his bones."

I didn't have the power to argue or resist. Weeks later, the pain subsided but my elbow didn't return to its normal alignment.

After I recovered from my injuries, I started saving the shillings again, and in time, I tried two more business ideas. For a sheep project, I bought a lamb from the animal market planning to raise it until it reached market value. That failed when my mother didn't send us money for Eid festivities, and my grandmother sacrificed my lamb for the celebration. And in my last venture, I planted sugarcane in the small piece of land in front of our hut, but nothing would grow.

With the failure of all my business ideas, I returned to dreaming, and to holding the reflection of my mother every morning in the mirror of my imagination, the same way my friend held his mother outside our school.

Absence would shadow me out of the camp, carrying along its power to evoke and instill creativity.

—Sulaiman Addonia

UP OUR SLEEVES

There's an idea going round like a rumor these days, consoling and heartbreaking at the same time. Some people dare to say it out loud, but a little guiltily, as though nostalgia were a slightly obscene luxury. They say: "We just want things to be like they were before." No question about it, this is the year we have most clearly, vividly, felt collectively toppled into the uncanny.

This feeling, or this anxiety—in 2020 the two words seem inter-changeable—makes even those who know that the world needs to change, who *want* the world to change, catch themselves by surprise by thinking what they would have previously found unthinkable: "We just want things to be like they were before."

We try to find this "before" wherever we can. Among our friends, for example. The other night, at a dinner where we greeted each other by touching elbows rather than with our usual effusions, my friend B. told me that her son's school had called her the day before. It was urgent. An emergency call from your child's school, in September 2020, immediately makes you think of fever, symptoms, quarantine . . . but no, B. told me, it was a "before"-style emergency. A hamster emergency. Her son had brought his hamster to school. He had slipped it into the sleeve of his sweat-shirt and taken it to class, where he eventually let it go, and the hamster had caused a disturbance (actually, wild excitement) among the students. Then it had scurried off I don't know where, behind a radiator, under a shelf. She told me all this while drinking an Americano (her favorite drink from "before"), and I loved the story but hid my joy, because underneath this seemingly trivial anecdote was a reproach. Yes, a kind of reproach, even if my friend B. would never have put it in those terms. Because I was the one who had given her radiant child the idea of hiding a hamster in his sleeve. I had told him through a screen, during confinement, that in elementary school my friend R. had come to school with his hamster and not gotten caught. This hamster was our collec-tive secret, our collective responsibility, and we had succeeded, not just once but several times, in evading the teacher's vigilance. Eventually, she ended up finding out what he had up his sleeve.

* * *

Thirty years separate these two hamsters-up-a-sleeve. This reassured me: how nice, how "same as before," I thought. Of course that's not true. In reality, these stories, for all their similarity, are not in the least the same. Why? Because our world—the constant change or chaos that our world has become—creeps in everywhere, even up children's sleeves with their hamsters. Because it was an experiment on hamsters last spring that proved the effectiveness of masks in the fight against the spread of Covid-19, and B.'s son and his friends knew it: with this little ball of fur, they were actually playing pandemic, reenacting and outsmarting it. The concrete meaning of the hamster in their imaginations is not the same at all. The hamster's more diffuse, long-term meaning in their imaginations is not the same either, because in these thirty years the European hamster has become a critically endangered species. When I was a child, the species was considered harmful. People hunted them. Now we are trying our best to reintroduce them, otherwise in another thirty years they will have vanished completely.

Domestic hamsters, of course, are not European hamsters, which don't fit in an eight-year-old's sleeve: they're bigger, tougher, and meaner, too. But if they do disappear, then the way we—our children, our children's children—perceive domestic hamsters will necessarily evolve. Just as our perception of cats will change when there are no more tigers or panthers in the world. (In what new way will we read *Moby-Dick* if there are no more whales?) Maybe that line, "We just want things to be like they were before," is what adults tell themselves because they lack the courage to slip a hamster up their sleeve: The joy of transgression. The joy of finding their joy—a fresh, sweet joy—in themselves. The joy of rejecting solitude, both our own and that of another little creature who depends on us. To play a game where you save the animal—where you save the world—might just be already to save it, a little.

—Jakuta Alikavazovic
Translated from the French by Damion Searls
First published in Libération *on September 18, 2020*

SOMEBODY

After my divorce, I lived alone in a basement apartment. The bedroom window looked up at the street through a concrete pit where garbage collected with seasonal trends. That February, it was blue paper cups. I invited over a stranger, who brought with him a glass pipe full of crushed diamonds. The stranger held a torch lighter to the bulb and melted the drugs into an amber liquid that we inhaled, night after night, for two weeks. I lost fifteen pounds, skipped class, and called Peter to come down to Brooklyn. *I need your help.* He'd never heard me say that phrase, and during the call he purchased a bus ticket to Brooklyn. I stayed sober for two days. The night before he was supposed to arrive, the stranger returned with that high that's so difficult to verbalize: a conversion of blood into light, an absolutely beatific lifting sensation, a divine boredom where time smoothly passes with fits of awe—even the barest ceiling lightbulb receives a halo, and turning water into wine feels cheap in comparison. Each ticking second of the hangover is a match struck against your skull. After the stranger left, eight hours passed, and I still could not stand without collapsing. My heart wacked out, and my vision failed and returned, and my hands received little electric shocks or went numb.

I called an ambulance.

On the ride, I called Asiya and told her I didn't want to die alone. She asked where they were taking me. The paramedic, who did not believe I was in any danger, watched me cry. Brooklyn Hospital. Asiya called a car to meet me in the emergency room. The paramedics seemed disappointed that I wasn't dying fast enough, or that I wasn't obviously dying at all. They thought I was wasting their time. Instead of rushing me into the hospital, the paramedics dumped me in the waiting room like used furniture on the curb, whispering to security and nurses. *Okay condition, might be salvageable, or maybe just junk.* The security guard called me to a woman behind a glass window asking what the problem was, and although I could barely speak, I said I thought I had smoked crystal meth many hours earlier, too long ago for my heart to riot. She didn't find this important. I bartered for respect: I was getting a master's degree, I taught undergraduate classes, I didn't eat meat! I had made a mistake by hitting the pipe for a week. All disembodied truth meant nothing. I was a lonely body, a gaunt man clutching his chest, shamefully subdued. They told me to sit and wait to be called. I wished I had never called emergency services.

Asiya

Asiya arrived with a wind, wearing a black coat and jeans, her hair pulled back, expecting me to already have been admitted as she approached the security guard. Asiya had a balletic, intimidating presence. The guard pointed at me and the color drained from Asiya's face, confirming that I looked like shit, and then the guard double-checked her face, as if he weren't certain this skeleton was who she cared for. His stoicism collapsed, as he escorted me to a nurse, where I repeated the story: pipe, time, heart, boom. What Asiya gleaned from my face this nurse learned from my vitals. The rest happened quickly. They wrapped a bracelet that misspelled my name around my wrist. Asiya followed me down a corridor to a central room. They asked me to piss in a cup that nobody retrieved. I carried it back to my seat as if it were a coffee.

"Tell me everything I missed," I said.

Asiya held out her elegant fingers, counting what I was missing in our world. She'd received her yearly review, where she was called icy for the third year in a row. *Miss Ice Queen, three years reigning.* Our weekly parties disappeared. Everyone asked her where I was, as if she were the only one who could reach me, and she told them nothing. She had forgettable dates. Men embarrassed themselves and sent her pictures of their dogs. Our friends having affairs still kept them going, although we sensed they soon would end. I felt a thudding pain. Asiya grabbed the nearest nurse who took me into the EKG room. The technician looked at my hands and asked what I was holding—*It's . . . piss*—and checked my heart. He phoned someone: three, two, one, and a gurney arrived, and I was attached to a shrieking machine. The nurse informed Asiya they were admitting me to the emergency room due to the cardiac event. Asiya and I both looked at the nurse, and she said, in the way a diner server might tell you that they've substituted your white bread for wheat, "Didn't they tell you the EKG showed signs of a heart attack?"

"Asiya," I said, giving her my password and phone, "text Peter. If I don't make it, please tell Peter I love him and my ex that I love him, and give my manuscript to John."

They asked me to stand. My heart rocketed off and I fell, as the nurse and Asiya held me up, helping me onto the vehicle. We reached the emergency room. Asiya sat at the foot of the bed. Each doctor that approached read my chart (I could see them squint, *crackhead*) and looked at her. Asiya became my humanity. As I received an IV, Asiya told me stories as she watched TV above my head.

Peter

Peter's trip took nine hours, bus to train to car to hospital, and he relieved Asiya of the night watch. I said goodbye to Asiya, who lingered. I didn't have the energy to thank her. I wanted to cry seeing her leave. I didn't know if I would see her again. Beyond the realm of this white alarmist room, I hadn't believed my heart would fail me, and I was scared that without her friendship the doctors would return to seeing the junkie. Peter took Asiya's seat, and he too watched the television above my head.

"What's on TV?"

"There's no TV," Peter said.

"What is it?"

"It shows your vitals."

"How do they look?" I asked. Peter—verbose, intelligent, funny—didn't say shit. He rubbed my leg and demanded the cardiologist, who spoke to Peter instead of me, as though he were my translator. They administered a medication to open my arteries. Peter rubbed my shoulders, whispered into my ear, as the medication took a flamethrower to those great chambers of being, and I screamed until my veins opened. When my heart rested, he fell asleep, head tilted back, jerking suddenly into consciousness, saying, *I feel like I travelled across the ocean.* I stayed awake as the wide-open veins prepared for some yet unknown passage, but I didn't want to wake Peter. A moment of rest, I could live for that long, I needed to give my friends what I could. They had created a portal through which strangers saw the world where I wasn't tomorrow's ashes, and I joined the hour of saving.

—Kyle Dillon Hertz

THE GUITAR

It was the first year of the great dying.

And while we didn't think it would be gone by Easter, that day when the great bear rolls back her boulder and reenters the born-again world of spring, we did tell ourselves that all the bad things would end.

It was a year, I think, in which some things bent, but did not always break. Though I also know now there can be great glory in the breaking.

It was a year I walked again and again into the old forest for strength, and something else. I walked carefully across the tops of fallen giants, the spongy carcasses continuing to give long after the trees themselves had all but disappeared.

What if for a tree, or any of us, there is no end, really, to the living?

The old forest at the top of the valley is where water first comes into Montana. Up here in the Yaak is as far north and west as you can go, and still be in this country. It's where the sun is last seen each day in this state.

Does a tree have a voice? Every living thing has a voice. Or should.

Of all the living creatures, wood has the best voice, for the voice of wood has a life beyond itself. Wood vibrates, resonates forever, physicists say, with all the sound it has ever generated or received. The wood has a memory.

Does it know what's coming?

It is said that the rain falls equally on the just and the unjust; and that may be true. But different angles of light fall differently on every object in the world; upon the living and the unliving. Some are gilded with it, others scorched. Some are starving for it and others may receive too much.

But water: everyone needs the same amount of water. Water, unlike light, can and does go away. The old forest up in the Yaak Valley is the place through which our first water flows—being distributed to the East Fork, the West Fork, the North Fork, and the South Fork; into Zulu Creek, Zero Creek, Mule Creek, Winkum, Midge, Hawkins, and so forth. It births, splays, Montana's first river, into outstretched shimmering radials of life. The old forest gives us all the water we could ever want; but in exchange, we *must* protect the temple where it begins. It originates in a mind-bogglingly complicated forest, but it's not a complicated relationship. It gives water; we give the old forest respect.

The light does not fall on us equally. Those at the top of a hill, for example, receive and bathe in it earlier and later. They have it both ways.

The sweet secret things down in the lowlands wait for justice. And wait. And keep on living. Like a voice caught forever in the wood.

A small group of us, the Yaak Valley Forest Council—rebels, poets, dreamers, scientists—has recommended the government create a climate refuge up here, in the far northwest of Montana, in the last place the ice left, long ago. It's the last place the fire will come to. We believe it's a place to study the effects of climate change, not a place to erase.

This one forest—what the Forest Service now calls Unit 72—there's no other way to talk about it but spiritually. Like Noah's ark, it still has at least two of everything. Salamanders, grizzlies, owls, lynx. Lions. Caribou, down from the north.

Like the Garden of Eden, this is a place that has not yet known the bruising hand of man. There are large parts of Unit 72—I prefer to call it the old forest—that have never known fire. The forest floats atop a perched water table. The forest guards the water just below.

What lies within the bark of these eight-hundred-year-old larch? In the assemblage of secret chemistries whirring at the base of giants might be more data than even our computers could handle. But we can listen for it. We can listen *to* it, and know it in that manner. It is a floating forest of hummocks and frost pockets, stippled with fairyland fens and miniature marshes. This old forest has self-regulated for nearly a thousand years by a little-known phenomenon called "gap creation." The forest feeds upon itself, and upon that light. Upon that water. When the spruce and subalpine fir become old, they crash down not like as if from an ax blade, before they are ready, but with a shower of light that is in step with time and reason: down through the overstory, creating a gap—and into that gap, the light rushes; and from that gash, life surges, as it did on the first day.

All of the seven days of Creation can be found in this forest, in any one moment. It is a great and perpetual floating orchestra of light and sound and life, and a kind of eternal dying that is not at all a dying.

Does color make a sound? Does the light that falls upon us? I believe it does: that the waves of light shooting toward us from the sun—rays sent out toward us so long ago we give them their own beautiful term, *light years*—create a sometimes unique and other times familiar sound, notes and chords as each wave shimmers and oscillates, each one sliding along against the others next to it. Some are silky and others, raspy; some are fragmented; others supple with the joy of the living. But yes, light makes music. Anyone knows that.

It is said among some communities in the far north, the aurora borealis make a sound that only children can hear, and that the northern lights can be summoned to come closer when children whistle back to them.

We—the Yaak Valley Forest Council—went in ahead of the devastation: ahead of the Forest Service's plans to clear-cut a thousand acres of ancient forest. The Forest Service had already begun the defiling; had painted their pitiful offering of "leave trees" in orange and blue, directing the sawyers where to go and not go. Only the garishly painted trees—one or two per acre—would be spared, though after all the others were gone, even the painted ones would die, unable to survive their sudden isolation. And meanwhile, the loggers would slay every other living thing that did not have the mark upon it.

We went in behind them, trying to undo the humiliation—a forest must stand together, or it is not a forest—but they kept coming back and painting over our paint.

A tree, much less an old forest, was not made to be painted.

The one we found—the chosen one—was big, but had taken centuries to get that way: 312 years, give or take a couple of sunrises. It would have been a single cotyledon at first, a sun-warmed seed—a single idea—with no sound at all. Who knows who its parents were? In that sense the guitar we make out of it will be an orphan too, but in another sense it belongs to all of us, for whoever hears its voice shall forever after carry that trembling, that music, within.

Before it came to us—before we came to it—this 150-foot-tall Engelmann spruce grew above a steep shaded bank through which a creek used to run, before the Forest Service gashed the creek to let it bleed out. All the subsurface water clutched by all the ancient roots seeped out into the gash and was carried away, down the muddy logging road, beneath the now-blazing sun. That slash is what brought a desert to the very edge of the old forest.

A storm had tossed the spruce over. When we cut the giant open—taking only a single vertebrae—we could *smell* the music that would come. Could feel it, even before the luthier first laid his hand to it. There was, and still is, joy in the wood. I guess that sounds funny—what does joy sound like?—but really, how could any living thing be in that forest for 312 years and not be comprised of joy, or even the thing that lies beyond joy? A thing we may not yet have a name for.

The tree had been lying down for a year when we came to it, but we could still feel the sound in it as surely as you could the heartbeat of an immense animal.

The growth rings were so close together. Like a closed fist, gripping the music—not letting go until we came for it. Until we were ready for it.

It felt odd, taking even a single piece of wood from that perhaps-doomed forest. Like all great things, it had a tiny hairline crack in its center; we could see that, once we went in with our tools. The wound had been held tightly almost from the very beginning. It was a shock to see that which some might think of as a scar or blemish, within.

What possible good can ever come from all this pain? The weakness; the spine around which the body wraps: the weakness that hides deepest within a person, within a tree, or a nation. Surely one day, surrounded by the slow music of time, that tree, or human, or nation, comes to think it is finally safe, and that the hidden crack is no longer a weakness. Has vanished.

It never vanishes. It just becomes hidden.

* * *

We bathed it with water from the river. We bathed it as if anointing it with oils, as we prepared it for its next journey. How long ago its birth seemed. The year would have been 1709. Europeans would have just arrived. Pilgrims, back East, wearing those funny shoes. Witches in pointed hats. Oh, wait, maybe they weren't witches, for when they were tied up and burned alive they did not unfasten their bonds and fly away. Though maybe they did. I hope so.

We've seen some things in this country, this tree and those of us who are still here. And all this time, it's been waiting to speak.

A virus is not a living thing. It's more of a mechanical thing, a scrambled sheath of proteins which, like a living thing, is just seeking a place in the world. Why are they in the world, why do they "want" to latch onto us, use us, get what they can from us, then move on to the next? That is perhaps more of a spiritual or even religious question than it is one of evolutionary biology.

It's not hard to identify a virus. It's small, sure, but you can see it under a microscope. A virus is and yet is not like an idea—*beauty*, say, or *wealth*: an abstraction, one where, when you look under the microscope, you see nothing. You can't see the idea, but it's gotten inside you.

We are trying to build a guitar from this ancient forest before the Forest Service, the Kootenai National Forest, erases it from the earth. Erases it from everything but memory. The wellspring, gone. Green wet life turned to hot dust.

They say that it, the clear-cutting, will make the old forest *resilient*.

They are saying the forest is in danger, and must be protected from itself. They are saying they know a way, with their bulldozers, to make the forest better.

This is the birthplace of the wild Yaak. It is also the place in Montana to which all life can retreat and take shelter during the great burning. It is the most beautiful place, and the most mysterious, and for both of these reasons, possibly the most dangerous: feared, reviled, by some.

It was the time of great dying, and the time in which metaphor went away. *I can't breathe*, the man kept saying. Speaking for all of us.

Have we become so accustomed to ugliness that we fear all beauty?

I am afraid of the answer. Again and again, I go into the old forest, while it is still here, more than an idea. I go there quietly, to listen. Everything trembles. Music was here long before we were. Listen. Listen harder.

—Rick Bass

LINA MOUNZER is a writer and translator living in Beirut. Her work has appeared in the *New York Times,* the *Paris Review, 1843, Literary Hub,* and *Bidoun,* as well as in *Hikayat: Short Stories by Lebanese Women* and *Tales of Two Planets,* an anthology of writing on climate change and inequality.

The Gamble

LINA MOUNZER

I remember the first night my father came to us and said: tomorrow we will be millionaires. We believed him. That was back when we still believed most of the things my father said.

We must have been in Montreal only a few days at that point, in that furnished apartment where the kitchen was not so much a kitchen but a counter overhanging one of the couches in the living room, and the living room was barely big enough to sit all five of us at once. The carpet in the apartment was an overcooked pea green and the curtains had large ugly flowers on them and the view was of a redbrick wall, though I didn't mind that part because it reminded me of the buildings on Sesame Street. My younger brother and I were still zinging off the furniture into the wee hours, sleepless with excitement and jet lag. Why do I immediately think of tiger stripes when I remember that night? We may have asked him if we'd be rich enough to afford a tiger. He may have said yes.

My father was a great teller of bedtime stories though he never told them often enough for our liking, because he was rarely present, or able, at bedtime. These stories were serials that each took place in their own universe, but there were tantalizing promises that they might spill over into our own. For example, there were the stories about Ringo fi bilad al bingo, where Ringo had adventures in the faraway lands of Bingo as he searched for his best friend, traveling from place to place looking for him in a great contraption that was essentially a ball inside another ball. The interior ball, with its captain's seat and gleaming, bleeping electronic dashboard, like the inside of a spaceship, stayed upright and steady while the outside one was transparent and coated with a scratchproof, dirt-proof polymer, so that Ringo could look out the front windshield while his vehicle rotated on well-oiled bearings, rolling over any sort of terrain: mountain, desert, and sea. My father took as much care describing the mechanics of that contraption as he did Ringo's various adventures, maybe more, because I remember that ball better than I do anything else about the stories. He promised he could, and in fact would, build us one of our very own. In Australia, he said at first, and then when it became clear we weren't going to Australia, in the United States, and then when it became clear that a US visa was going to prove impossible, in Canada. We believed him. We believed almost anything our father said because he was a genius. It's not just that our mother repeatedly told us that he was a genius; we could see it. My father could draw an eye that looked so much like an eye you kept waiting for it to blink, and he could play the violin and keyboard, and could fix the keyboard when it short-circuited by welding tiny wires to other tiny wires, and he could do math sums in his head, and he read fat science fiction books by Isaac Asimov and talked about space travel and faster-than-light vehicles and how the future would be a wondrous place of shuttling back and forth between the earth and moon. "Your father could have been anything he wanted," my mother would say. An artist, a scientist, an inventor. If only, if only.

Growing up, everything I knew about the past, personal and historical, was inflected with that melancholy of the perfect, rendered in the grammar of regret. It was not just my father's bright dreams that had been thwarted by the fates—it was this whole region into which we'd been born. Had it not been beset by occupation; had it not been claimed as a spoil of war by the British and French; had they not signed declarations and agreements that carved up the territory as they saw fit, sidelining our own leaders, installing rulers, and making way for settlers as they pleased; had they not, with all this, crushed any hopes of sovereignty and self-determination. Had our liberationist movements been given an honest chance to succeed; had our best and brightest not been imprisoned or assassinated; had every dictator and despot and occupying force not been given arms and financial support and moral backing for the most egregious crimes against humanity by the United States or else the Soviet Union. And in the midst of it all, there was little Lebanon, every utterance of its name always accompanied by lamentation, either in tone or word. Ya haram ya lubnan, oh, poor Lebanon, once so beautiful and cosmopolitan, with its ancient ruins and modern cities, its snow-capped mountains and deeply blue sea. So many resources, so much potential, had the French not crippled it from the outset with a system of governance that meant success and positions and hence money were only attainable not on the basis of merit but on sect and connections alone. Had it not, by virtue of its location and famed openness become the proxy battleground for greater powers near and far. Had this not meant that it, too, would be rent apart, tearing at the weak seams that had been sown into its fabric from the very beginning.

In the face of such great forces, arrayed against you from the outset, what could save you? Certainly not will alone. It could simply never be strong enough to power you through. What was required, rather, was wit. Cleverness. You had to take the unexpected path between these giant obstacles. You had to take bold risks. You had to outwit the fates, because you couldn't fight them head-on. They were too big.

My paternal grandfather taught every one of his eight children these lessons. Born on the bottommost rung as far as both sect and class were concerned, he died—after years of swaying wildly between fortunes good and bad—in a middle-class home, in a middle-priced bed. He'd pulled himself out of the muddy fields he'd been working for a pittance since the age of seven by teaching himself how to read and write, which eventually helped him make his way out of the valley, up the hills, and down the mountain into the great port city of Beirut, where he found a job peddling gas from a donkey cart up and down the length of the old Sidon road. He would move from Beirut to Baghdad to Tehran and back, his brood of children, and hence mouths to feed, multiplying along the way, chasing the right connection that would lead him to the right business deal that would make him rich forever, and, as the Arabic expression goes, "bury poverty for good." But things would never quite work out in his favor. In Baghdad, the cargo of sugar in which he'd invested all his money, that was certain to make his fortune, sank in the river before ever docking. In Tehran, the mass arrests following the US-orchestrated coup against Mossadegh included his business partner, and he had no choice eventually but to pack up the family and leave.

I didn't learn any of this from my father, nor did I ever know his feelings or his place, as the eldest of the eight, in any of it. I sensed only the burden of it, embodied in the halting vocabulary of his movements and gestures: the expectation that he would have to do even better, depart even further from the position in which he'd been born. In no other way, however, did my father ever speak of the past. Instead, he was a great believer in the future. For himself and the world at large. It was the promised land where everything we'd ever wanted would come to be. It was his favorite tense. When we are; we will; we'll have; you'll see. I used to think that belief in a shining future was a way of refusing to dwell on the failures and disappointments of the past. A form of resistance to it. Now I think the opposite. I think the past and future are the same place, taking long refuge in either the same thing. A way of avoiding, not living in, the present.

Here's the one true thing I know about my father's childhood, one of the rare things he told me himself: when he was eleven, or fourteen—no one seemed to remember exactly—he survived a fall from the fourth story. He had just showered and gone out onto the balcony to hang his wet towel. Somehow his hand touched one of the wires that crisscrossed the narrow skies in such neighborhoods. This wire happened to be live. The current grabbed hold of his body and flung him clean off the balcony and down onto the pavement below. Is that how it happened? Is such a thing even possible? In any case, he fell from on high, and against all odds, he survived. He survived, even after the doctors told my grandmother that she had better call the sheikh and begin preparing the shroud. He spent months and months recovering. His jaw was shattered and had to be wired shut for the better part of a year. By the time I knew him, the only physical trace left of it was a thin, crescent shaped scar on his chin, white against the brown of his skin. His upside-down smile, I called it.

My father hated religion, hated mumbo jumbo: he believed in science. He saw religion as the purview of the dull-witted, those who weren't brave enough, intellectually speaking, to strike out into the unknown. I also think it's because religion necessitated a belief in fatalism, in the idea that everything that comes to pass comes to pass because god has written it so. This meant that the future, too, was already decided, as irrevocably locked-in and unchangeable as the past. And when the past was all doom and defeat, the highest probability was that it foretold the same about the future. Thus, no one wishing to make their way forward and upward in the world could afford the indulgence of such a thought. To shed a belief in fate was somehow to shed the weight of the past altogether.

And yet, despite his rejection of what he called nonsense, my father also had faith in the strange, random, improbable, and unpredictable possibility called *luck*, which is different from the set of fortuitous circumstances referred to as *privilege*. A lot of what looks like luck on the surface is in fact, upon further scrutiny, privilege. And my father, though he would never learn of that particularly modern word for it, knew very well how to recognize privilege, for there is almost no one to whom it has been denied who cannot identify the halo of its blessing—always hovering above someone else's head. But luck, real luck, can happen to anyone. Real luck, in fact, is the only wild card that can trump privilege.

This possibility, I think, is what my father gambled on his whole life, even as he convinced himself that beneath it all was simply a code of probabilities that could be cracked given enough determination and smarts.

If my father's beliefs sound contradictory, that's because they were. All addicts exist inside a contradiction, at an unmappable crossroads between the forces of fate and individual will. Fate (genetics, circumstance, hard luck; not I) made me an addict. Will (power, determination, pure self) will allow me to overcome it. Perhaps that's why twelve-step programs, instead of employing linear logic to lead people out of addiction, simply flip this contradiction around. Will, choice, made me an addict. Surrendering to a higher power—not I—will allow me to overcome it.

My father was a happy drunk, or at least, the drink undid a sort of tightness, heldness, around his eyes and mouth, and this made him appear happier. When he was surrounded by people, as he was back in Beirut, he was only one of many drinkers in the evening. His voice would ring out from the living room and into the bedroom I shared with my brother at the end of the hall. We'd listen to him tell stories to other people, regaling *them* with his quick wit and clever ideas. There would be roaring laughter and the slap of cards, or else the clatter of dice on the back-gammon board. My father was equally loud and good-natured in his exclamations whether he won or lost. He never, ever let the resentment of the sore loser dull his tone, but he definitely always played to win. Even when he couldn't manage to gather a large group together, there was always someone willing to share a drink and a laugh and a game with him in the evenings, as often as shelling or checkpoints would allow.

It took a long time for the facts to add up, for me to even think the word, *alcoholic*. There were many reasons for this, the most obvious being that drunks on TV were mean and violent, all their held-back ugly thoughts torrenting out the minute their lips were loosened by drink. My father was the opposite. When he was drunk was the only time he let himself express, with abandon, affection or love. "I love you so *much*, Baba," he would gush. Encouraged by his mood and words, we'd ask him if we could, say, take a trip to the mountains that weekend, or if we would have a swimming pool in Canada, or if he could finish tomorrow the story whose ending we were dying to know. "Of course, Baba," he'd say. "Tomorrow you'll have anything, everything you want." We believed him. Only later, after we'd been in Canada for a while, would we come to understand that when he smiled like that, blinked like that, smelled like that, he never really meant, or even remembered, what he'd said the next day.

Many things were revealed in Canada. I suppose, in that way, Montreal was exactly the fresh start it was intended to be. The strike out into new territory, the bold move West, where each of us could be free to realize our potential, taking any road we pleased, without the countless restrictions that narrowed our possibilities back home. Everyone knew anyway that Lebanon, the entire Arab region ya haram, was a lost cause—there was no future for anyone there. We left behind the civil war, all its fear and commonplace horrors and discomforts, and went to a place where waking up to see the next day was a certainty rather than a question of odds. My parents bet everything we had—the money we'd saved, yes, but also our friends and family and language and geography and weather—on this flat, cold, very cold place where they had no idea that the system was gamed against them from the start. Where connections and insider knowledge and perceived class were just as important as they'd been back home, only in this new place my parents didn't understand the underlying rules that governed them. Where even the cleverest person could be deemed stupid, slow-witted, and unfit for the level of employment their experience qualified them for if they were struggling to master a third language. And where, cut loose from all support systems, it was revealed that those alone had been propping up the illusion of a happy family, more or less united in cause and purpose. We fell apart from one another like so many loose twigs and my father, always slightly at a remove from us, always slightly unattainable, retreated into his own world entirely, lost in his own calculations. As though living in a parallel timeline. A hologram, there in body only, like a character from one of his science fiction novels.

With the fates arrayed against him, you see, my father was not about to let them win. He was going to outwit them, take the unexpected path, the shortcut that would shoot him past all the obstacles and into the shining future he'd dreamt of all his life.

My mother says he was pretty much hooked from the very first night. We'd barely put our bags down, so to speak, in the furnished apartment on Boulevard de Maisonneuve before he went across the road to the dépanneur to buy milk (and also whiskey, and cigarettes), and returned with a fistful of lottery tickets and shining eyes, asking my mother if she knew, could she even *guess* what the grand prize was for the person lucky enough to win the pot?

And that was the other reason it took me so long to identify my father as an alcoholic. It was that his drinking problem was the least of ours.

My father claimed he had a system, that he could crack the code of the numbers. It was all a game of probabilities. He would go no farther than this in his explanations. He would sit at the dining room table, at which we never ate because it was always covered with papers, and all the papers covered with columns and rows of numbers, some of them with little sketches and caricatures of people he knew in the margins. He bent over them like a medieval scribe, writing out numbers in his neat hand, sometimes punching furiously into a calculator.

Occasionally he would quiz us on our dreams, listening for anything that resembled a number.

"I dreamed I was being chased by soldiers!"

"How many were they?"

"I dreamed I was older and living alone."

"How old were you?"

"I dreamed we traveled back to Beirut."

"What was the flight number? How many passengers do you think there were on the plane?"

"It wasn't on a plane, Baba, we just suddenly appeared there, and we all liked it much better than here."

The lottery results were always read out at some point late in the evening, between 10 p.m. and midnight. Close to the magic moment when today becomes yesterday, tomorrow becomes today. My father would have spent all day poring over his numbers, smoking cigarette after cigarette as he filled out the lotto cards carefully, circling six, or was it eight, numbers out of sixty-nine, barking out reprimands if anyone got too loud and distracted him. At some point in the late afternoon, after taking a break to watch *The Simpsons*, which was the only activity we did together, he'd leave, his one outing of the day, to go to the dépanneur and hand over money we didn't have, money he'd borrowed, to exchange those cards for electronic versions of themselves, where the choices were made irrevocable. His fate sealed. Then, if he happened to be out of whiskey, he'd go to the SAQ and pick up a bottle—Black Label when he wanted to splurge, J&B if he couldn't, the same two brands he'd drank in Beirut. He'd come home, and pour the first glass out for himself, settling into the living room couch, his head hunched over the Game Boy, which he'd bought for my little brothers but quickly claimed for himself. He was especially good at Tetris, calling us over excitedly to see the pixelated celebrations when he beat all nine levels, doing it so often our enthusiasm quickly wore into eye rolls and sighs.

When the hour came for the results he would always stand, never sit, in front of the TV. Onscreen there would be a man and woman, the man in a suit, the woman in a lovely dress or tasteful skirt. The very picture of respectability, both. Nothing sordid or hopeless here. The man and woman would be on some brightly lit stage somewhere against a stark white backdrop, the logo of the provincial lottery behind them. A great transparent ball would turn, like Ringo's magic ball, filled with smaller, colored balls that bounced crazily about inside, sometimes revealing flashes of numbers. Then they'd roll out of a tube on the side, one by one, and the woman would hold them up, smiling maniacally, her long nails gleaming, while the man read the number out. What feral, furious, ferocious optimism must have gripped him as he stood there, waiting! He never betrayed any hint of it, only sometimes swaying slightly, but that also could have been the drink. I can only now imagine what must have bounced and roiled behind his set features: possibilities as bright, as wild, as buoyant as those dancing balls. In that moment before the first number came out he was always a potential winner, always seconds away from an eternally changed life.

What did he think he would win?

What did he imagine he could afford to exchange for that money? Our house, surely; the car. The country in which we now lived? The expectations that had been placed on his shoulders from the outset, being the eldest of eight, being so smart, being now the unwilling patriarch of his own disappointing family? Perhaps he thought he could exchange all of us for happier versions of ourselves. Perhaps he imagined he'd wake up the next morning, and, rich, we would all be thinner, gleaming, well-behaved. A family of whom he would no longer be ashamed. For this is what he blurted out one day—stone-cold sober—when my mother confronted him during one of their many house-shaking fights, asking why he couldn't be more present, why he couldn't set the lotto cards and whiskey bottle aside for one goddamned day so we could all go out together as a family, enjoy the things we'd left everything behind in order to be able to enjoy, namely parks and open spaces you didn't have to pay for and afternoons that could unfold at leisure without chaos or curfews. "Because," he said, "I am ashamed of all of you." We were not the family he wanted. We were not the family he ever had in mind.

Here's a thing my father blurted out to *me*—drunk as a skunk—late one night when I was the only one around. I forget what prompted it; most likely nothing. My father's conversations and confrontations were all with himself. We just sometimes got to hear the odd snippet of all that mental chatter, on the very, very rare occasions he let his guard slip.

"*You*," he slurred, pointing unsteadily, "you don't know what love is."

I remember my breath catching, both enthralled that my father was trusting me with something adult and also terrified of what he would actually say. I was seventeen, molten with first love, ablaze with feelings I was certain no one else on earth had ever felt or would ever feel or could ever understand, so great and grand and sublime were they. My father knew nothing of this, of course. He went on:

"*I* know what love is. I know love like you can't imagine. It makes everything possible. But maybe you can answer this: If a man has been able to experience the kind of love that makes everything possible, but then he loses it, does that make him lucky or unlucky?"

Hard-core gamblers are always willing to stake everything on the bet, but can rarely pay up their losses. To avoid the acceptance of loss you must be ready to gamble again. And again. And again. It's like any other addiction. To avoid reckoning with the price it has exacted from you, you must continue allowing it to return you to that place of refuge, from where it is possible to dream that this is it, the last time, the final plunge before a triumphant emergence. From inside addiction, sobriety seems like the place where all your possible selves can come true. But sobriety itself is a slog, because it is a place of daily reckoning. It unfolds minute by slow minute, in the present simple. The only place where a real sense of the future—the future continuous—exists is inside addiction, that magic moment that comes every day, when you decide to succumb for the very last time. And so you surrender to your fate, assuring yourself that it was, in fact, an act of will.

In any addiction, the debt you incur is always owed to yourself; the debt you incur is that of time. You borrow from the future to forget the past, to make the present easier to bear. Tomorrow you will be the winner. Tomorrow you will pay it all back by living as fully, as happily as you can.

When all the givens were aligned just right, my father could be extraordinarily fun to chat with. He did hilarious, merciless impressions of all the Lebanese people that Canada had forced him to befriend for lack of any other options. He whistled distorted versions of famous tunes and tried to get us to guess what they were. He was always making jokes and puns by creating mixes of Arabic with English with (terrible) French.

His favorite thing to talk about was how technology would solve every problem humanity ever had. He spoke confidently of the day when computers would be small enough to be carried in people's pockets wherever they went; when robots would take over all the hard labor and save so much time and money that it would shift the culture from one where people had to work to live to one where they could pursue whatever they damn well pleased. He liked to speculate how there were probably entire other universes inside black holes, where life was so different we couldn't even imagine the rules that governed it.

He was especially wildly excited about the internet. Said he'd predicted it all along. A global information network that would make laughable all borders. He died shortly after it came into our household. In the era of Netscape and Hotmail, long before Gmail or Yahoo. After the paramedics left our house, while my mother waited for the sheikh to arrive, to perform death rites my father would have rolled his eyes at, I sat in the basement and listened to the keening howl of the dial-up and then tapped out an email from our AOL account to my friends back in Beirut, who were all spending the summer together without me. *My father just died of a heart attack*, I wrote. Or maybe: *My father just died. He had a heart attack*. Something as short and sudden and quick as what had taken place that August morning in an upstairs bedroom of our house. I couldn't tell if I was being overdramatic in my wording or not dramatic enough.

For the longest time I didn't know what to feel. Or rather, I could not identify any of the sharp specifics inside my general, awful sense of loss. My father had not so much left us as completed, made visible, an absence that had been present among us all along. He had postponed the business of living until he'd simply run out of chances and time. Anyone could have seen it coming. Anyone could have predicted he'd die of a heart attack. He ate badly, smoked too much, drank too much. What strains, too, that nightly anticipation must have placed on his heart. He hoped too much. He wanted too much. He carried more sadness than should be allowed and never shared it with anyone.

But even while he was actively killing himself, I'm sure he never truly believed in the possibility of his own death. For there are many like him who don't die. Who carry on, despite all odds. Who survive the first heart attack and go on to live better, healthier lives, having been scared straight. There are also others who do everything right, and then one day collapse just as suddenly and finally to the ground as he did. There are those who trip on a step and fall at such an odd, improbable angle that it kills them instantly. And there are those who fall from the fourth story of a building after having been electrocuted and live to tell the tale.

I don't know how he mythologized that survival for himself; how he explained it in his own vocabulary of belief. I know my grandmother said it was because god had decided it was not his time to die. I know that my grandfather said it was because he was clearly destined for a great future. I also know that when my father tried to kill himself one drunken night before I was born, it was by attempting to throw himself off the balcony before he was wrestled down into submission.

But he did not die either of those times. Instead, he died in Canada, in a bedroom of our suburban house where we were behind on rent, far from anywhere he considered home, almost exactly three weeks shy of his fifty-fifth birthday. He died and left us to sort through piles and piles and piles and folders and boxes of papers scrawled with numbers, an incomprehensible code known only to himself. And with forty thousand dollars in credit card debt.

When someone dies, the only way to give condolences in Arabic is to hope that, despite all this, god smiles upon the future. There is no way to say, "I'm sorry," or "my condolences." It seems ridiculous, in fact, to offer up the smallness of individual contrition in the face of this, the grandest of all things. There is no "I" in any of the words offered up as consolation to the living over the departure of their cherished dead. Each dialect of Arabic has its own call and response for this occasion. A rote script that also gives the grieving something to say back, when they might otherwise have no words. In the Levant we say, "el 'awad bi salemtak." May the compensation for this loss be found in your own health. Or else, "el ba'iyyeh bi 'omrak." May the lost years of the deceased be added to your own life. The Syrians say, "inshallah khatimat al ahzan." May this be the last of all your sorrows. And the response for all of these is to wish the blessing back, always accompanied by some variation of "inshallah." If god wills it. Death is the greatest of obstacles, the strictest and most unchangeable of fates. It is the single certainty, written from the start. In its face, this truth must be acknowledged by all. When it comes to death, a surrender to fatalism is a great comfort. Otherwise the *if onlys* might shackle themselves to your feet, tripping you back into the past every time you try to move forward.

Years later, long after I'd left my mother and brothers in Canada and moved back to Beirut, as I'm sure my father would have wanted for himself if he'd had the chance, I was flipping through one of the countless photo albums at my grandmother's house. I went through them every time I visited, always paying close attention for sightings of my father. Rare were the photos in which he looked truly happy; even as a child his face was guarded and full of sorrows. One day, I came across a picture of him with a woman so white-blond the blob of her hair was almost like a burn in the black-and-white photo. She wore a mod little dress and thick-framed glasses. My father looked both shy and terribly pleased with himself.

"Who's that?" I asked my aunt.

"Oh," she said, as though I knew this, as though she and everyone else had not been keeping this from me my whole life, "that's your father's first wife, Anke."

My aunt wouldn't really tell me more. Every question I had— How long were they together? How did they meet? Did they have kids? What happened, why did they divorce?—was met with either a shrug or the briefest and most untelling of answers. It would take many more years to piece together what had happened, and even still I don't have any clear picture. The only person who was forthright with me about it was my mother, but even she was never allowed but the smallest, blurriest glimpses into my father's past or inner life.

They were together for two, three years at most. She was Dutch. They fell in love when she was married to someone else; she divorced him and immediately married my father. They were crazy about one another. They had no children of their own but she had a young daughter from her first marriage. His family disapproved. They never said so outright but made it icy clear. She was foreign, divorced, older. He was the eldest; he was expected to shoulder the heaviest of the family's expectations, the entire weight of all the sacrifices my grandfather had made to give them all a better future. My father was torn between loyalty and love. He was given, not in so many words, a choice. He chose wrong. He regretted it for the rest of his life.

In North America my father became openly taken by the idea of individualism: that a man could be whatever he wanted, that his fate could turn on a dime (or a million), that he alone was responsible for his success. "You are the master of your own destiny!" crowed any number of the sparkle-toothed maniacs he liked to watch on TV. "Today is the first day of the rest of your life!" And he believed them, or at least I know he wanted desperately to believe them, I think because that would have been the ultimate way for him to make a fresh start, to prove that he was truly able to leave the past behind.

But none of these wild-eyed gurus, the chanters of North America's siren song, ever mentioned the way a person could be fettered by circumstance; acknowledged that one could be anchored to the weight of family or country or class or body or war or history in such a way that made it not only impossible to attain success by being the master of one's own destiny, but outright ridiculous to even think it possible. Those weighed down the heaviest would have to muster all the forces possible to be able to pull forward: will, yes, inhuman will, which is what this philosophy mandates—but also cleverness, brilliance, wit, talent, and even then, none of these might ever lead anywhere without the magic boost of that powerful, unpredictable little engine called luck.

But as I assess the lost potential of my father's life, I always find myself asking: Where is the line drawn between personal responsibility and collective circumstance? Between fate and individual will? Between irrevocable past and open future? Between the hand we are dealt, and how we choose to play it?

This line, like the present moment, is a slippery thing. Ever-shifting, ever-changing, moving elsewhere as soon as it is grasped.

My father would have hated me writing this, hated me revealing anything about him at all. But where does a person's jurisdiction over their own story end? Is it with death? Or is it when a person has children, and their story becomes essential to the way someone else might understand themselves and their place in the world?

In every sense, my father's story is also mine, and that of my brothers. It is both the burden we carry, and the material from which our own fates are made. Each of us can only try and chisel it for ourselves into a shape less severe, both for his sake and ours, but its facts, now that he is gone, are set in stone.

I am old enough now to understand this very simple truth: that because my father's story is my own, to be compassionate with him is to be compassionate with myself. Likewise, to hold him to account is to also do the same for myself. And again, I find myself lost between poles, between distinctions that might be obviously identifiable to other people but which have always been so difficult for me.

A view that I hope maintains some balance, calibrated to the lesson I wish most to take for my own life: my father was dealt a mixed hand, but what hindered him above all was that he was a fearful player. He was also never allowed to reveal that fear, not even to himself. Being a man, being an Arab man, being a man of his time and place and origin, he was not permitted to ask for help; he was not permitted to fail. As such, he never let himself take the boldest risk of all, which was to bet on his own talents and see where they might lead. He saw his cleverness only as a means to an end, a tool that was worthless if it didn't produce wild success, and wild success, for him, could only be measured in money. He rarely allowed himself the simple pleasure of creation, just to see what he might make, or what it might make of him. He rarely, in fact, allowed himself any pleasure, except the pleasures of addiction, which come with harsh punishments built into them. He had, like many people—like me when I don't catch myself—a simplistic view of what it means to win, and what it means to lose. As though life has some final score, some moment of arrival at a finish line that isn't death.

I wish there were a system to follow, a code that could be cracked. But I wouldn't even know how to go about finding it. My beliefs, like my father's, are a contradictory mess of cold logic and riotous feeling, of magical thinking coupled with disdain for certain kinds of faith. Like my father, I carry the vast histories of my region and my country, as well as the smaller histories of my family and myself, each of them inflected by tense, aspect, mood, and voice. Out of this chaos I must every day try and make a story to best serve my purposes. That is all I can do. I know that what I write today is not what I would have written yesterday, nor is it what I might write tomorrow. I might regret the things I've revealed, or the things I failed to say. I am choosing to write it regardless. The only real truth that can ever be told, anyway, is that of the continuous present.

Künstlerroman

OCEAN VUONG

After walking all night on the trail, you make it to the wooden gate.

It's locked, of course.

On the other side, children's voices, finally happy.

Beside the gate, on a schoolhouse desk, is a beige TV set from the 80s.

The kind with the VHS player attached.

Taped to the desk is a card that reads: *You must rewind before going further.*

You have nothing left, it so happens, but the cassette in your hand.

You push it in and the screen flicks on, revealing a man in a pressed black suit standing before a wooden gate, pointing at a television.

You press REWIND and the man walks backward, through a pine grove littered with dead needles, then a field of poppies, past a ravine choked with cars rusting from another century.

He walks backward through the night-green hills, hands in his pockets. The crescent moon, like an empty boat, skims the sky.

He makes his way to town, up the steps of the grand hotel, into a hall crowded with crystal chandeliers, ceilings frescoed with angels, satyrs, and unicorns. Waiters with plates of coconut shrimp, flutes of champagne. The room a kingdom of light.

The man is surrounded by merry people in fine dress. They whirl backward around him, their faces flushed with opulence. The tie he wears is the one his cousin Victor gave him outside of Drew's package store, saying "You're a writer now, you should look like one" three weeks before Victor checked himself into the psych ward at Silver Hill.

One by one the people hand the man a book, the artifact of thinking. He opens each one and, pen in hand, traces a deliberately affected, illegible signature, until the name, in red ink, evaporates. Everyone raises their glasses, satisfied, their mouths open as crickets intensify all around you, the screen flickering as the tape whirrs.

He walks backward through the crowd, alcohol flowing out their throats into glasses as he leaves the hall toward the empty streets, alone.

He walks as the sun rises. Days, weeks, months of walking.

You watch him hurry through airports, convention centers, dip into taxis, even a limousine, then a governor's mansion, through immaculate rooms of leather-embroidered divans and marble mantels, Tiffany lamps, polished granite counters, rooms just for "sitting" where no one ever sat. Fresh fruit piled in teak bowls set to rot.

On the screen, you see dust shoot up from the surface of a river, then gather into a massive cloud under a bridge, before funneling into the copper urn in the man's arms.

His face looks unfinished. The man's little brother rests his head on the man's shoulder. In their oversized, rented suits, they look like ambassadors from a country no one remembers.

You see him leave yet another mansion, down the long driveway flanked with phlox and geraniums, down the pitch mountain road at night, along dirt roads of towns whose names you hear only when a hurricane passes through, gas stations overgrown with ragweed and asters, past an alley wide as a fat man's face, over gravel medians where somebody's father was last captured on CCTV. You see him enter the basement of a row house with eight satellite dishes jammed on the garage roof, the sound of needle wrappers torn open, the occasional face from high school, thirty-two-ed and sucked out under a two-second match.

You can't hear but can feel their laughter in your hands, the way a voice bashed against a wall turns to dust in your bones. He feels the rush like a new spine as the warmth of junk makes him true.

Cigarettes spark in the dark like fireflies in a jail cell.

You watch him stop by the cornfield (where he once lost his dog, Cheetah, and sat for two hours in the corn crying in another tongue) to pick up his suit jacket hung on a broken hydrant. He puts it on and heads backward toward his mother's house, where he kisses her on the cheek in a grimy kitchen, the $50 bill going from his hand to hers, then back into her bra. He heads up the stairs, into the bathroom, and lets the vomit in the sink return to his mouth. Snot back up his nose. Hands shaking.

Time does not heal. But, forced backward, it repairs.

The tape skips—now you see him lying on the floor in a dimly lit room, his eyes shut, tears leaking down his ears, darkening the hem of his starched dress shirt.

He blows his nose, rises to his knees, hands over his face. A framed medal, some ornate award, floats into his arms. He kisses it, searches the glass for his face, then gets up, flicks on the lights.

He's in a dressing room, surrounded by mirrors. His red, wet eyes on every wall.

He walks backward through double doors, through shafts of light, the award tucked under his arm. Down a wide linoleum hall, through a foyer where reporters flank him, cameras, forced grins, stiff handshakes, half hugs, then he steps onto the wing of a stage in the opera house, the crowd roars mutely, the award raised with both arms, its gold edges glimmering under ethereal houselights. His heart a fish tossed into the wooden boat inside him.

The tape skips and you see him walk backward out of the Stop & Shop on Griswold, the one that starts to crumble, brick by brick, as he gets further away. Bulldozers, men in hard hats—until it's razed to the ground, then replaced by larger, irregular stones, becoming the walls of a century-old church, the steeple rising under the wrecking ball's touch. Pieces of stained glass gather into Saint Francis's haloed face.

He walks backward into the church, Kelvin's casket glows in the dusky light. Mothers and grandmas with heads bowed. But what he wants, or rather, what you want for him, doesn't happen: underneath Kelvin's button-up, the pink eye in his chest, just above his right lung, doesn't open, the .45-caliber bullet doesn't come out, won't suspend itself in September's cobalt air, won't make its obedient return to the barrel, splinter into lead, polymer, iron, elements, the ash of a star ejected from a cosmos into this one.

Kelvin doesn't sit up in his casket to kiss his father, Mr. Rios, on the forehead when the man hobbles by to put a Tonka truck in his nineteen-year-old boy's hands.

The dictator on TV, the noose removed from his neck as the world watches. The dictator crawling backward into the hole in the ground, his face crumpled law.

You keep your finger on REWIND, like a good citizen, and the man in the suit keeps running backward through the ruins you've made for him.

Summer approaches spring as he walks, freshly nineteen, into a motel room off Route 2, where clothes come off like bandages. He lies very still on the lumpy bed beside a soldier, just back from the desert, with a missing right ear. The light from the street falls into the hollow where the ear once was, making a medallion of gold on the side of the man's head. The boy puts his tongue there and waits to be forgiven.

56

On the wall, the shadows of their erections fall, then rise. We are rare in goodness, and rarer still in joy. Their clothes come back on, like crumpled laws.

He walks backward as the soldier walks backward. They smile at each other until both are out of sight. The night returns to itself, less whole. The Maybelle Auto marquee a beacon in the fog.

Books disintegrate back to trees as the tape roll thins. The trees rise to their feet. The drugs leave the veins of four friends in the Mazda, the car flipping nine times on I-84 and landing on its wheels, their necks re-boned to their lives as they sing Ja Rule and Ashanti, eyes shut in a freshman hope.

The "lol," "lmao," the dick pics vanishing from AOL Chat screens, the "asl?," "are you a virgin?," "can you meet right now?," "are you down?," "are you Asian or are you normal?," "can I be your dad for an hour?," "do you know how 2 love yet?," "i can get a room. u can do ur homework while i work on that ass," "are you there?," "hey i won't hurt you," "call me," "faggot," "I need you," "fuck you," all of it gone from the screen into binary code.

And the gypsum, calcite, and lead dust rise from the pavement in billowed clouds, and the North Tower becomes itself and September's clear and blue, and the people float up to stand looking out of windows in good suits, in good bones.

The tulips raise their heads, their chins high along the courthouse lawn.

The tanks roll out of Iraq, the women backing away from their dead, rags over their mouths.

The tape scrambles and you see the boy dancing with his mother in the front yard in the '97 nor'easter, snow hurled to the sky as he twirls under her shadow—cast larger than life by sodium lights. The flakes going up and up to thicken god's pillow for his never-ending sleep.

Then the ice retreats, the ground beneath him red and ochre as if an enormous mammal had been opened at his feet. And the leaves rush in the gusts, attach themselves, by thousands, to oak branches across the yard. His mother, at the window, lifts her head from her hands, eyes drying.

Then you see the boy walk backward into his house, lift his mother off the kitchen tiles. His father's fist retracts from her nose, whose shape realigns like a fixed glitch. If you slowed it down here, you could mistake the man's knuckles for tenderness, a caress. The way you soothe something with the back of your hand so it won't fall apart. The father backs away, out of the kitchen.

The boy lying under the branches of a blue spruce, screaming.

You see him float up the tree, like a puppet on string, back to Kelvin's hands pressed to his back, both of them laughing.

Then the cake on the table, air returning to the boy's pursed lips as the seven candles, one by one, begin to light, and the wish returns to his head where it's truer for never being touched by language.

The children's laughter louder now—but cut with static, as if played on a record just beyond the gate.

You are starting to root for him, on his way to dust.

The family howls, ecstatic, on the lawn, their arms waving in the summer night. The son, clutching his Elmo, dances in circles as they all head inside, where the mother picks up the phone: she's gotten a job at the clock factory in Meriden.

The Hubble telescope swoops the other way. Halley's Comet shoots back behind the trees as the Humvees roll, once more, into Iraq.

You watch him as he passes an empty carnival where a tobacco field once greened. It's the day after the Tri-County Fair, you can tell, where all that remains of October are sunken pumpkins along the road to the city jail, the clowns sitting on stools behind their trailers wiping away makeup in pie-tin mirrors. The cornfield husked and rattling in the breeze, the highway beyond the pines with its air of gasoline and burned rubber. He walks backward though there's so little time left to destroy. Backward until he bowls over, on his hands and knees. Until he's crawling on his belly like a soldier with a missing ear, his grey Champion hoodie browning in blotches, soot appearing, like mold, on his cheeks, neck, fingers. His jeans fall away in crisp pieces as he drags himself down the road where he made his name. A thin line of blood appears along his jaw.

Soon all that's left are his tattered boxers. He crawls, half naked, his arms covered in cuts, toward where the smoke is rising from the ditch by the road. When he gets there, he slips his feet through the mangled rear window of the Corolla, fastens the seat belt, turns his head toward the concussion, and waits for the glass to reassemble, for the friends in the front seat to sing again.

He is saying something. You slow the tape down to read his lips.

No, not words—but laughter.

You look down at your shiny dress shoes, the pressed black suit.

The children's voices a memory now.

You press EJECT and realize your hands are already his hands. And he's using them to pull open the gate.

As it swings, you glimpse, through the widening crack, what was there all along, your hand over your mouth.

And all the wrong answers, like you and I, go back to being good questions.

SAYAKA MURATA is the author of many books, including *Convenience Store Woman*, winner of Japan's most prestigious literary award, the Akutagawa Prize. Her latest novel to be translated into English is *Earthlings*. Murata was chosen for inclusion in *Freeman's: The Future of New Writing*, and was a *Vogue Japan* Woman of the Year.

GINNY TAPLEY TAKEMORI has translated fiction by over a dozen early modern and contemporary Japanese authors. Her translation of Sayaka Murata's bestselling *Convenience Store Woman* was awarded the 2020–2021 Lindsley and Masao Miyoshi Prize. Her translation of Kyoko Nakajima's Naoki Prize–winning *The Little House* was published in 2019 and of Sayaka Murata's *Earthlings* in 2020. She lives in Japan.

Final Days

SAYAKA MURATA
TRANSLATED FROM THE JAPANESE BY
GINNY TAPLEY TAKEMORI

I guess it's about time, I thought, and decided to go ahead with the preparations. First I contacted the workers to dispose of all my belongings.

"Are you making plans to die?" a young man asked.

"Yes. Either tomorrow or the day after."

"Really? My girlfriend and I are thinking of dying together next month or so."

Many couples in their twenties or thirties chose to die together. "How nice," I said automatically.

"May I ask what setting you have in mind? Disneyland, I imagine. Or a meadow of flowers?"

"No, I have a more natural death in mind."

"Oh wow, nice. A natural death. That's what my sister did, too."

The young men went about their work chatting cheerfully until there was nothing left in my apartment.

"Well, that's us done. Have a good death!"

I picked up my backpack, the only item left in the empty place, and went outside.

About a hundred years had passed since medicine had advanced so far that nobody died any more. Nobody aged either, and even if you died in an accident or were murdered by someone, technology was such that you could immediately be resuscitated.

It was feared that the population would explode, but surprisingly that hadn't happened. As it was, once we thought we were ready to die we could do so in whatever way we liked. Bookstores were full of volumes on ways to die: *Perfect for Women! 100 Cute Ways to Die*; *Die Like a Man! How to Leave an Impression in Death*; *The Top Ten Ways for Lovers to Die☆Illustrated*. I myself chose one titled *Let's Die Naturally! Super Deaths for Adults & the Best Spots*.

The right time was different for different people. There were some who had reached two hundred years old and intended to keep going, while some children died when they were only ten. I'm thirty-six now and I don't know if that's early or late—I just somehow started to feel that it was time. My hunch was probably right, though, since the population remained steady at about the right number without increasing or decreasing.

After flicking through the book and getting a pretty good idea of what I wanted, I went to city hall and filled in a do-not-resuscitate order to ensure that even if my body were found, no measures would be taken to revive me. Once that was done, I dealt with other practical matters such as what to do with the little savings I had, and obtained my death permit. The formalities were more complicated than I'd anticipated, and by the time I finally finished and went outside again it was already dark.

I presented my death permit at the pharmacy and asked for a relatively strong, fast-acting drug so that I wouldn't suffer.

"You take care of yourself, now. Have a good death!" the young woman pharmacist told me, throwing in some vitamin tablets free of charge.

I got onto the night train and headed for the location described in the book. It was a quiet place deep in the mountains. In the winter it was a busy ski resort, but in this season the only people here had come to die.

I alighted at the appointed station, and headed off into the mountains on foot in search of a quiet place. On my way I passed by a couple stabbing each other with knives. A lot of couples chose killing each other as their way to die. I skirted around them, taking care not to get in their way. After walking along the mountain road for a couple of hours, I finally came across a deserted spot with a lovely view that looked like a nice place to die. Following the instructions in the book, I dug a hole with the spade. Maybe someone else had been here before me, for the earth was soft and it was easier than I'd expected.

When the hole was ready, I lay down inside it and drank the mineral water containing the drug I'd been given. Then, while still conscious, I began covering myself with earth. I couldn't do it as thoroughly as someone else would have done it for me, but still I managed to get myself more or less buried in the ground.

Breathing through a short hose connected to the surface, enveloped in the warmth of the earth, I closed my eyes. Before long the drug would take effect and I would die buried there in the ground. Returning to the earth like this was currently a popular way to die.

I didn't want people gossiping about me after I was dead, laughing about the way I died or commenting on how I was so plain in life but then chose a flashy death causing problems for others, or saying that I should have known better than to die like that, and so I wanted to go as quietly as possible, a classy kind of death.

Before medical care had become so advanced, death had apparently been something that came unpredictably. A drug would be the best way, I thought, given that I would have to bury myself. I wanted my death to be as unobtrusive as possible.

Suddenly my head grew heavy, and I knew I was dying. Wouldn't it be great if natural deaths were restored in the next world, I thought, squeezing my eyes shut, and then abruptly lost consciousness.

ALEKSANDAR HEMON is the author of *The Question of Bruno, Nowhere Man, The Lazarus Project, Love and Obstacles, The Making of Zombie Wars, The Book of My Lives,* and *My Parents: An Introduction/This Does Not Belong to You.* He is working on his next novel, tentatively titled "The World and All That It Holds," as well as a work of nonfiction, *How Did You Get Here?: Tales of Displacement,* that was the recipient a PEN/Jean Stein Grant for Literary Oral History in 2017. Hemon is the winner of the 2020 John Dos Passos Prize. He cowrote the script for *The Matrix 4* with David Mitchell and Lana Wachowski.

The River

ALEKSANDAR HEMON

> If one thinks of pain as a dam
> that impedes the narrative flow . . .
>   —Walter Benjamin, "Storytelling and Healing"

The night before Walter Benjamin was
to be returned from Portbou to France
and into Nazi hands, he understood:
Being alive doesn't mean you've survived.

His uncle told him a story once:
A man was teaching his horse to live
without eating, and, just as it learned,
the horse died. It was funny at the time.

The morphine pills he would swallow,
he counted more than once. He hoped
he would be carried light, along a river
of stories, all the way to its big mouth.

Caresses would mark the wide riverbed,
while everything on the way to the sea
of blessed oblivion would be swept clean,
until he finally dissolved into being, home.

ADANIA SHIBLI has written novels, plays, short stories, and narrative essays. Her latest novel is *Tafsil Thanawi* published in English as *Minor Detail* and a National Book Award finalist. Shibli is also a researcher in cultural studies and visual culture, and teaches part-time at Birzeit University, Palestine.

CHRISTOPHER STONE is Associate Professor of Arabic at Hunter College of the City University of New York. He conducts research on Arab popular culture and is the author of *Popular Culture and Nationalism in Lebanon.* He has previously translated literary texts by Adania Shibli, Najwan Darwish, and Muin Bseiso for publication.

A Bright and Ambitious Good-Hearted Leftist

ADANIA SHIBLI

TRANSLATED FROM THE ARABIC BY
CHRISTOPHER STONE

The United Transport Company stands alone on a square kilo-
meter of land in the heart of Jerusalem. It is bound on the west
by street number 1, which falls on the line that divided the city
into East and West Jerusalem in 1948. To the east are the Garden
Tomb and Schmidt's girls school. To its south is the Jerusalem
Hotel, and to the north lies Damascus Gate, which leads into
the old city. Here one usually finds large and small white buses
with green lines on their sides on which is written, "The United,
Jerusalem – ", then the name of the area where that particular
bus is headed. In the eastern part of the bus station sits a small
building with a lounge for bus drivers and an office where the
company's founder and majority shareholder usually sits. "Ra'ed
al-Tawil," as he is called on official documents, is the eldest son
of Umm Ra'ed and Abu Ra'ed al-Tawil. While only his wife and
a few family members call him Ra'ed, everyone else calls the
company's founder Abu Arab.

In the early nineties Abu Arab fell in love with a girl from
Jaffa, a beautiful girl, except perhaps for her prominent jaw. This

girl, however, did not reciprocate Abu Arab's feelings, which naturally saddened him. He first met her on one of the trips from Jerusalem to the Sea of Galilee that leftist students used to take in the small bus that he rented out and always drove for just such occasions. Abu Arab had bought the bus to support the family after his release from prison. His mother had sold all of her gold jewelry so he could buy it. Abu Arab had been a "security prisoner" for two years because the Israeli authorities suspected him of being a member of the Popular Front for the Liberation of Palestine. His father had preceded him to prison on the same accusation, then another brother, then the next, and then the next. When, one night, the Israeli army raided their house in one of Jerusalem's overcrowded neighborhoods and asked Umm Ra'ed about the whereabouts of the remaining brother, who was twelve, she beat the soldiers to the room where this brother was sleeping and started kicking him while shouting, "Get up, Mr. George Habash, get up!" At that moment the head of the military unit intervened and saved him from her. Yet later, the investigator resumed the kicking with such intensity that that brother confessed to having thrown stones at a military patrol. His classmate, however, never confessed, a fact that has left his soul deeply scarred.

The bus project turned out to be a success. Soon after buying the first bus, Abu Arab was able to get another one for his brother for when he got out of prison. The brother drove workers, whereas Abu Arab continued to drive university students and sometimes journalists or artists, something he really enjoyed. Even though, after prison, Abu Arab had given up completely on the idea of finishing high school, he still felt sad about it. And perhaps this sadness increased when he realized that the college girl from Jaffa did not like him, and that perhaps no left-wing college or cultured girl would like him, because he had not finished high school and was just a bus driver. Eventually, however, the women of the family met and decided to introduce him to another girl, a cousin named Abla, who just happened to look a lot like the first girl. The two immediately fell in love, though perhaps Abla loved him a bit more. Abu Arab, in turn, introduced her to his intellectual and artist friends. She was shy with them at first, but his close friends soon got to know her intimate and gentle side. Also at the beginning, because of Abla's family's reservations, Abu Arab was not able to meet with Abla alone, though he so much longed to. Instead, Abla's grandmother, the family's supreme authority figure, always had to chaperone them. Thus the grandmother also met Abu Arab's university and intellectual friends, who were able to soften her up and convince her to leave Abla and Abu Arab alone by themselves. Her only condition was that they tell no one. Therefore I ask the reader to keep this fact a secret, even though the grandmother died a few years ago, and now Abla and Abu Arab are married and have seven children, six girls and a boy.

The first child is Kamilya. Abu Arab named her after his friend Kamilya Jubran, the lead singer at that time of the group Sabreen, of which Abu Arab was a huge fan. Kamilya is a beautiful girl who studies at the Rosary School and Abu Arab can't wait for the day she goes off to university and he sees her standing at the Qalandia checkpoint on her way from Birzeit University back to Jerusalem. As for the second daughter, Karmel, her name was chosen on the way to the maternity hospital in Talbiyya, on the road that divides East and West Jerusalem. Everyone liked the fact that she was named after a Palestinian mountain and that the name began with the letter "K" like Kamilya's. Abla and Abu Arab, however, knew that they couldn't keep up this pattern of names starting with the letter "K," for as soon as they had a boy, they were going to name him Farid after Abu Arab's father. Therefore, they dropped the "K" names after Karmel's birth, which was an extremely difficult one. While giving birth Abla began to beat Abu Arab and to scream, "It's all your fault!" It saddened Abu Arab, who held onto her hand, to see Abla in so much pain, which he was helpless to stop. That day they thought they might not have more children. But luckily the following births were easier. Karmel is a beautiful and smart girl who studies all the time. As for Farid, he's a gentle and intelligent boy who loves his six sisters a lot, perhaps with the exception of Aya, who is a year older than he. She's also not so fond of him. This might be due to the fact that Farid is a highly sensitive child who feels gratitude towards those who love him, whereas Aya couldn't care less about that and seems, rather, to be completely consumed by her curiosity towards the world. The other three are still small. The oldest of them speaks somewhat slowly, giving each and every letter its phonetic due. This could be because of a fall she had from the second floor two years ago. The ambulance took forever to come, as usually happens in the case of Palestinian injuries. That day, Abla felt a great hatred for the whole world, including herself and to some extent Abu Arab, since it had never occurred to him to encourage her to get a driver's license. The time she spent waiting for the ambulance was among the most painful in her life, more painful even than giving birth to Karmel. However, it's a good thing that Abla didn't have a driver's license at the time, for she was hardly able to stand on two feet that day.

It wasn't a problem for the family that the little one spoke somewhat slowly. They gave her all the time she needed, especially since Aya's rapid-fire speech, which really annoyed Farid, saved them so much time. The two smallest ones still cannot talk. They are fraternal twins, but if one did not know they were siblings, one would never guess that they were even from the same city.

Abu Arab and Abla's ambitions were not limited to expanding the world's population, but also expanding their own company. And, generally, the number of buses they owned grew with the number of children they had, until they eventually possessed five small buses. Then Abu Arab suddenly thought about selling them, along with a small plot of land the family owned in Bethlehem, all for the sake of a new project. But his efforts to convince his parents, and especially his siblings, failed initially. According to them and to many of his friends and acquaintances, it was a completely crazy idea. Abu Arab, though, was not to be deterred. He decided to carry out the plan on his own. He sold his share of what the family agreed was his after years of tireless work, which came to two small buses. Then he sold all of Abla's gold without telling anyone (and I ask the reader again to please keep this information a secret). Abla not only loved Abu Arab, but also believed in him. Objectively, though, the idea, which was to buy the Ramallah-Jerusalem bus line itself, seemed like something only a crazy person would support.

The line was owned by the Ramallah Bus Company, which had remained in operation until the beginning of the 1990s, after which its buses stopped running and the company disappeared completely. Before that, its service had been limited to running two old and run-down buses that no one dared ride except for those who had both no money and all the time in the world.

It was, then, only a few senior citizens who used the Ramallah-Jerusalem buses, and occasionally students who couldn't pass up the chance to procrastinate between home and school. But this wasn't the main problem. The main problem was that even fifteen years ago, these buses were run-down. Now they were more like worthless archeological ruins. The second problem was that there was no longer a direct road between Ramallah and Jerusalem that buses could use even if they were able to make the trip in the first place. The road had been divided into several sections in years past, what with checkpoints and the wall. So now everyone, including the senior citizens and schoolkids, definitely preferred the shared taxis that were quite fast. Quite fast, that is, when they were actually moving, which gave the rider the sense, even if illusory, that they were moving at the fastest possible speed after however many hours of waiting at the checkpoints.

Last but not least, the idea was also crazy because Abu Arab did not possess a license to drive large buses. In fact, neither he nor any of his brothers ever would. According to Israeli transportation law, former "security prisoners" were barred from obtaining the license needed to drive large buses. In short, he and Abla threw all of their hard-earned savings into something that no longer existed, and, in fact, could not exist in the future. But Abu Arab looked at the situation differently. While all of this was true, Abu Arab could see beyond the present circumstances. For him, the success of any project depended on the possibility of the creation of different circumstances in the first place.

So, Abu Arab started down this path all by himself, spending long hours in the garage where the buses had been lying like sick cows, trying to fix what could be fixed. He repainted the buses and reupholstered their seats. After several months of work, the two buses began running again. One of them ran from Ramallah to the Qalandia checkpoint and the other from the Qalandia checkpoint to Jerusalem, even though their signs said that they went from Jerusalem to Ramallah. The phrase "Jerusalem to Ramallah" was like words on a gravestone, a reminder of a life that no longer existed. In any case, at least now a route that had been dead for a long time had come back to life, even if a limited and partial life. These two buses slowly got more and more attention from riders, and not only because they had been refurbished or because they saved riders something on transportation costs, which had become exorbitant thanks to the breaking up of the road to and from Jerusalem into small segments, but also because people believed that the drivers of the small buses were a pack of thieves, drug dealers, sexual harassers, and even collaborators. And even though no one scrutinized these claims very closely, the drivers' behavior did nothing to help their reputation. Thus the popularity of the Ramallah-Jerusalem buses rose every day, especially since the buses left at scheduled times and not just when they filled up. And it rose not just among the passengers, but also the drivers, who respected Abu Arab as the lawful owner of the route which many of them currently used unlawfully.

One day Abu Arab, who as already mentioned in the title, was a bright and ambitious good-hearted leftist, called for a meeting of all of these drivers. His suggestion was as follows: as a bus owner he, like them, wanted to ensure his and his customers' safety and well-being. This required that they unite and work together. As everyone knew, he was the owner of the Jerusalem-Ramallah route, but that was beside the point. What he was suggesting was that the owners of all the buses that used this route join his company, which would be called, instead of the Jerusalem-Ramallah line, the United Transport Company. As the sole owner, founder, and investor in the company, he would hold fifty-one percent of the shares, dividing the rest among the drivers who joined the company, which they could do without investing any money. All they had to do was join with their buses, buses that would remain their property, not the property of the company. The company would simply be an umbrella bringing together all of the bus drivers and owners to ensure and protect their rights, as well as the rights of the passengers, especially in the face of the Israeli authorities, who were constantly harassing the drivers of small buses. All the bus owners had to do was provide accident insurance for their passengers and adhere to the ticket system so as to be able to pay the taxes levied by the Israeli authorities. They would also have to make sure that all drivers wore the same uniform so that it would be easy for the passengers to identify them, and agree to standardizing the colors and signage used on the buses in line with the logo of the company of which they would now be shareholders.

The number of members of the company increased day after day until all of the bus lines leading to Jerusalem had joined in, a situation the passengers were very much in support of. And finally, Abu Arab's family came around to the project.

Naturally, Abu Arab still cannot drive any of the large buses that he owns or that fall under the umbrella of his company. But at least he owns two cars. One, an old jeep, he drives when he goes on long trips with his entire family. The second is nothing special, something he uses to take the kids to school every morning on his way to the office, where he remains until late at night, making sure that any problems connected to the company are on their way to being solved.

SANDRA CISNEROS is a poet, short story writer, novelist, essayist, and visual artist whose work explores the lives of Mexicans and Mexican-Americans. Her numerous awards include a MacArthur Fellowship, the National Medal of Arts, a Ford Foundation Art of Change Fellowship, and the PEN/ Nabokov Award for Achievement in International Literature. Her novel *The House on Mango Street*, which has sold over six million copies and been translated into over twenty-five languages, is considered a classic. A new book, *Martita, I Remember You/ Martita, te recuerdo*, will be published in 2021.

A Boy With a Machine Gun Waves to Me

SANDRA CISNEROS

Maybe he is the same
age as the forty-three
from Ayotzinapa,
burned and buried
like trash.

Dark of skin perhaps
the same as the Atotonilco
man arrested and jailed
after a gunfire exchange
he did not begin,
in front of his own,
in front of his home.

Or in collusion with those
who abducted the blind
girl from Parque Juárez
and abandoned her shell
on the road to Celaya,
wrapped in a blanket,
forever in a field of sleep.

He's in the back of a jeep
with other boys. They
could be a baseball team.

Instead dressed
in black uniforms,
on their way to work
with machine guns.

I was coming from the market
with a basket of eggs
and a round loaf of bread,
a *xoloitzcuintli* perched
warm in the crook of my arm.

By Callejón de los Muertos,
their jeep rumbled past.
So many sons armed
with guns like toys,
though I know they're
real because I've asked.

Before they disappear
from view, my hand
raises itself as if
asking a question.

From the back of the jeep
a hand without a machine gun
answers back.

ZAHIA RAHMANI is one of France's leading art historians and writers of fiction, memoir, and cultural criticism. She is the author of a literary trilogy dedicated to contemporary figures of so-called banished people: *Moze* (2003); *"Muslim": A Novel*; and *France, Story of a Childhood*. The French Ministry of Culture named Rahmani Chevalier of Arts and Letters. As an art historian, Rahmani curated *Made in Algeria: Généalogie d'un territoire*, a large exhibition of colonial cartography, visual culture, and contemporary art at the Museum of European and Mediterranean Civilizations (MuCEM), Marseille, in 2016. This essay comes from the catalogue of that exhibition. Rahmani is currently curating the traveling exhibition *Seismography of Struggle: Towards a Global History of Critical and Cultural Journals*.

MATT REECK is an American translator, poet, and scholar. He won the 2020 Albertine Prize for his translation of Zahia Rahmani's *"Muslim": A Novel*. He has won fellowships from the Fulbright Foundation, the National Endowment for the Arts, the PEN/Heim Translation Fund, and during Spring 2021, he served as Princeton University's Translator in Residence. He has published seven translations from the French, Urdu, and Hindi.

Algeria: Held in Reserve

ZAHIA RAHMANI
TRANSLATED FROM THE FRENCH
BY MATT REECK

In France, it's rare to read an article about Algeria that isn't negative. And this has been the case for many years. In the end, we accepted it and moved on. Yet we have scarcely bothered to question this state of affairs, and it might be worthwhile to ask why. The members of my family who have gone back to spend time in Algeria, despite everything, and those who have come to visit us here tell two different stories. Without joy or pain, Algerians managed to make the land theirs, a land they didn't have the chance to call their own for long stretches of their history. What did we expect from them? How are they to live? After the independence movement and the failure of international socialism, we've watched with regret the country's many missteps. We wanted it to be a good, democratic actor, in keeping with the mandates of the French state. European, then? I don't know if the country itself ever really wanted that. And it's true that we haven't read anything good about Algeria since then. I'm not talking about the work of researchers and artists who are trying to bring to the surface another form of knowledge, another historical truth that, there, was ours. What should we think of this flood of texts in the French media that never stops wanting to capture another reality? "A seething mass of young people that don't know what to do, and that knows next to nothing," a French philosopher recently wrote on his blog. What does he know about this mass of young people who, according to him, knows nothing? After what the war against society, I mean, terrorism, taught these young people, the statement's ineptitude is striking. Who are these people, then, these citizens, these men and women, bound to ignorance or permanent unhappiness? Where do these clichés come from? And how could we be so well informed about this country, which is visited by so few foreigners?

As a child, I tried to find books to read about Algeria. I didn't find any. Outside of the stories my parents told, I didn't find anything that could teach me about the place I had come from. In metropolitan France, the end of French Algeria put an end to Algeria itself. A curtain fell over this country. And with it all of those men and women who left the country fell into the abyss. My family arrived after my father's imprisonment ended, in 1967, in a village in Picardy, a cul-de-sac abutting a marvelous forest. My sisters, my brothers, and I had just lost our country. We couldn't imagine finding it again one day. It was the price of our departure, we used to say. My mother understood the ravages of this mute sadness, that of the irremediable loss of the country of childhood. Whether it was due to the nearness of nature, or the reassuring fortress of our house, she never stopped transforming this world behind us, this hinterland of sensations, into fertile, luminous ground.

The scholars who undertook the scientific exploration of Algeria after 1840 never found the time to capture the full power of the oral tradition, including its political dimension, which for decades, for centuries, had been transporting the geographic, historical, and physical story of the Maghreb to madrasas, one pilgrimage after another. There was a time when all the peoples

Research photography for the video *Tracing a Territory, 2006*. Courtesy of the artist and kamel mennour, Paris (2006) © Zineb Sedira. All Rights Reserved, ARS, New York / DACS, London 2021.

of the world weren't separated on maps. Animals, people, trees, and rivers were all major parts of these maps. The Americas, like the faraway China of Marco Polo, were represented on maps with all of their palpable diversity but without any hierarchy. Animal ferocity and human violence were side by side with natural beauty, extraordinary birds, naked human bodies, and the jouissance of living. To look at a map of Guillaume Le Testu is to learn how people once used to live in the world. It's a little like looking deeply at a painting by Brueghel and understanding both the poetic force and the psychic density of what we have been given to look at. It was the same for North African maps. Kindred spirits, men and women shared everything in a seamlessly knit nature where the reign of the animal and vegetal bordered that which had been domesticated by humans. I learned very early what an antelope was, what a lion, panther, falcon, partridge, gazelle, ostrich, and, astonishingly, what even an elephant was. My mother would create stories about these animals from having heard them described, though never having seen images of them, or read about them, in a book. To recall these animals as though they were still alive, present in her childhood, surrounding her— as with her story (told in the present tense) of the death of the last North African elephant, which had in fact disappeared from those parts so many centuries before, or the fable-like stories of the dense and majestic forests in which people would talk to the shadows—was to maintain a living memory of Algeria that conquest had covered over and destroyed. While books weren't a part of my mother's life, her tongue was undaunted when it came to making sure we knew the ways of men and women, and their stories. Time, like chronology, was muddled. No verticality, no past, everything alive, and an elsewhere without limit. Moses and Abraham shared the same space as Maryam (Mary) and Sidi Aïssa (Jesus), her son; and the mother of Christ, who was all sweetness, would watch serenely over us as we slept. Likewise, the Prophet Muhammad would visit us in our dreams, brought by the angel Gabriel on his flying horse, which, by the immaculate white of his spread wings, would make us see the beauty of the world and its shores. She had received this gift of knowledge from her family, who had received it from their ancestors, who had received it in turn from theirs. Like that of the millions of women not allowed to attend school, her knowledge of religion and culture had benefitted from what the oral tradition taught about the uses of translation. It's worth remarking that the denial of formal schooling forced women to perform acts of translation capable of accessing the centuries-old modalities of the so-called oral languages. If reading is interpreting, to write is to materialize the text, to make it an object, an archive. A truth. And the text can show itself to be authoritarian and lawmaking. This objectifying quality of written language is absent from the oral tradition, and the latter has long been the source of resilience in Algeria. The oral tradition certainly played an essential role in the refusal of a large number of Algerians to send their children to French schools, which rejected all forms of multilingualism. To abandon your language is also to lose your culture. And what remains when the fairy tale, the fable, disappears? When only the book remains? And when you know that this book isn't yours? Edward Said wrote that in an empire, whether English, French, or some other one, only one language exercises the authority of knowledge—the language of the empire. There is only one language in empire.

We know that to translate is to transmit. But to transmit what someone else doesn't understand can lead to misunderstandings. When something doesn't exist in another culture, it also won't exist in its language. At best, I can describe it to someone. Point to its function. But as long as it remains foreign to the other and their culture, it can't be named. Which means that while the thing won't have an equivalent in the language of the other, it will keep its original name. Arabs (were they all Muslim?) came to North Africa, and we normally describe this exodus of more than a million people in terms of a quest for fertile terrain. They were accepted only by the grace of what translation made possible. The inhabitants of the Maghreb didn't speak Arabic. Then, after so many military conflicts, agreements, and apostasies, a compromise was reached between beliefs and things. And what had been there was able to meld with what had come, and what had just arrived was able to meld with what had been already there. We've hardly taken into account, up till today, this experience of the translation of the Maghreb. And we can now see, stepping back, that there were very negative consequences. In the nine-teenth century, it wasn't in the interests of French colonialism to valorize social practices born from the syncretism in place in North Africa. French military conquest and colonization rejected and neglected models of government that, through the centuries, had permitted the co-existence of the multiple political faces of Algeria. And if the word "tribe" was bandied about ostentatiously in the language of the colonizer, it was done so that the colonizer could circumscribe aboriginal peoples within a communitarian, tribal origin stripped of all competence and all legitimacy for self-governance. However, in this region of the world, Islam was marked with the rich cultural strata that had shaped the area over time. And landscape drawings of this territory, with its fertile zones and its arid areas, can only be understood as a superimpo-sition of European-Mediterranean forms of knowledge on top of those originating in Africa and the Middle East. Still, it's possible to think that the diversity of religions, the continued existence of ancient languages, the plurality of profane practices, and the power of myths shaped a being-in-the-world unique to the inhabi-tants of this region. Indeed, while there were many spiritual com-munities in Algeria, their schools were just as many. We must try to imagine what translation meant to this region. Across the coun-try, translation participated in a constant practice of mediation, negotiation, always in the service of a will to set aside, perhaps through attrition and the memory of past military conflicts, what violence the foreign could bring about. This place in the world, south of Europe, in North Africa, along the Mediterranean, had known so many invasions that it's entirely possible to imagine that its people had a unique attitude toward the question of the foreign. From cultural and geographic studies, Hanoteau's, for instance, we know that there was a well-established legal tradi-tion in Kabylia.[1] The violence of the invasion and destruction of

Algiers, and the incessant military campaigns, and the speed with which colonization took place, wiped out the legal codes that had existed beforehand and to which the archives attest.

The collapse of the cultural and legal–religious structures of not only Muslims but also the other inhabitants of Algeria took place while a radical, puritanical, fundamentalist Sunni strain swept through the Middle East. In opposition to the major forms of Islam at the time, this strain would return Islam to a narrow, doctrinaire form. In the adjustments and symbioses that had marked the spread of Islam across the world, Wahhabism only saw heresy. Let's not forget that Sufism, with its lofty spiritual goals, grew out of Islam's long and slow spread around the world. It was welcomed in the Maghreb. Wahhabism wanted only to do away with this kind of Islam. Many contemporary research projects study the linguistic and cultural diversity of Muslim Africa, and they show that this diversity is proof of the monotheistic faith's plurality, which, despite everything, still exists today. In North Africa, this insistence upon difference is also a way to keep alive a history and a memory of the experience of a form of translation vouching at once for the Arabic language's power of seduction and evocation and for a religious practice lived outside of its language of origin. The masterminds of colonialism very quickly took advantage of this cultural and religious diversity. Arabs, Jews, Moors, Kouloughlis, Touaregs, Kabyles, and Turks were all trapped in schemes of human hierarchization and separated from the indigenous populations to whom were applied, in most cases, the code of *indigénat* that was destined to make the indigenous populations whatever the colonizer wanted them to be. Men and women who would never have the power to decide their own future in their own country.

To convince yourself of the madness of this enterprise, all you have to do is refer to the texts (and they're easy to access) that are devoted to the defense of Algerian colonization and of its attitude toward the local populations. It's rare to find a land that has given rise to such an onslaught of publications and pseudo-scientific anthropological ramblings. No one listened to anyone but themselves. Officials, often aristocrats, very often the same ones who would become the owners of large colonial estates; military officers who were at times sincere Orientalists; men of the cloth; writers; businessmen; and philosophers—they all gave free reign to their views, which were often lethal. On this subject, we know what Victor Hugo and Tocqueville have written, but other than these, there were so many anonymous writers, like this man testifying to the Council of State, who while pleading for the total destruction of the inhabitants of Algeria, notes that even if "Algiers is a macabre legacy, an onerous possession, and we would be happy to get rid of it once and for all [...] we must be very certain about our patriotism in order to dare say to a people, 'You should stop your invasion.'"

It's enough to spend some time with the texts of Louis-Philippe's Africa Commission of 1833–1834 to understand the absolutely irreversible character of what had taken place in the first years, no, the first months, of the invasion. The violence of the French army and those under its command, the murders and the destruction, were so pronounced and so unexpected that they gave rise to permanent resentment in Algerian memory. The Commission, aware of this disaster, launched inquiries and interviews, and it attempted to evaluate the functioning of Ottoman Algeria and learn ways to establish a better relationship with the population. Yet, even for a French historian of Algeria like Xavier Yacono, writing in 1966 for an article in the *Revue de l'Occident musulman et de la Méditerranée* (*Review of the Muslim West and the Mediterranean*), the "results" of this "systematic study" had only ever been "partially put to use." What he includes of the reports filed by the king's advisor Alexis-Jacques-Louis-Marie Lhomme de La Pinsonnière, who was entrusted with the production of a report on colonization, aren't lacking for shocking details. "An Arab," says de La Pinsonnière, "as smart, lively, and even-tempered as he is, nevertheless has, in certain parts of the country, too much independence, too few needs to make him a good worker." Yacono writes that "while de La Pinsonnière's report is very critical of the behavior of the army and its attendant politics, he seems less pessimistic about the possibilities of progress for Algerian peoples." Yacono cites the report: "'We ask European colonists, while we're surrounded by many types of people in Africa, why can't we find in the indigenous populations all of the elements of colonization? [...] they have their own civilization, and we couldn't be more wrong to compare them to the savage peoples of America.'" Yacono observes that de La Pinsonnière was "unsparing" in his characterization of the situation:

'You stood before them, announcing loudly that you would bring them the benefits of enlightened society and freedom; they could have replied to you that they had had co-teaching schools for centuries, that all Arabs knew how to read and that it was your peasants who languished in ignorance [...] that it would be useful to have a newspaper; Arabs, naturally curious, would read it eagerly, especially if the contents weren't about religion, but rather about industry, agriculture, and other useful arts. Almost all Arabs know how to read and write. In each village, there are two schools. [...] They replied to you that without needs, and always being near a field for their herds and a spring to quench their thirst, they were freer than you, burdened by imperious needs of the social order that you wanted to impose upon them. [...] To submit these peoples to our social order, to tie them to the land, to make them into regular agricultural, industrial machines and taxpayers, would be such a beautiful and improbable result that we can only consider it to be a chimera.'

A chimera is a harmful, fantastical creature. So what should we think about the man painted in the foreground of the painting by Horace Vernet, "Prise de Bône, 27 mars 1832" (1835)? Seated on top of a wall that is under an infantry attack, he looks out over an immense, lush landscape. He seems entirely unaware of what is happening. The Orientalist school would say that he is lazy. We would say impassive. Yacono's footnote quoting a report filed by the Duke of Dalmatia reminds us that in 1831 the government in Algiers offered scholarships for Algerian children to attend French royal schools, yet "'only one person took advantage of this offer. Rather pronounced forms of loathing seemed to prevent families from handing over their sons to our schools. It wouldn't be without interest to learn the source of this repugnance in order to find a means to destroy it.'" In 1987, Ahmed Zir made *Repères*, a short, profound film on this question of deep loathing. Scarcely occupied, this country had been torn apart. Destroyed to its very foundations.

Fifty years after the war that led to Algerian independence, it seems that this country, represented in so many images and stories, reserves the right today of no longer engaging in any form of representation at all. So it's difficult to call it a tourist destination. Algiers and Tipasa aren't by any means banned. The Paris metro, magazines, and travel agencies have for a long time urged travel to North Africa. The sweet image of an oasis or *riad* brings to everyone's mind Tunisia or Morocco. Further to the east, it's the banks of the Nile and the Sphinx that we visit. So few have found a way apart from the strictly enforced tourist itineraries so far from social realities, which, inevitably, seem to respond to a very contemporary necessity. During a time when a perverted tourist economy made us believe again in hidden paradisiacal locales, fatigue led Europeans to see in a place only what they had already made of it. That's why people have loved Tunisia and Morocco, countries that we believe we know. For Algeria, it's different. Because while Algeria was a colonial laboratory, it was dedicated as much to agriculture as to tourism.

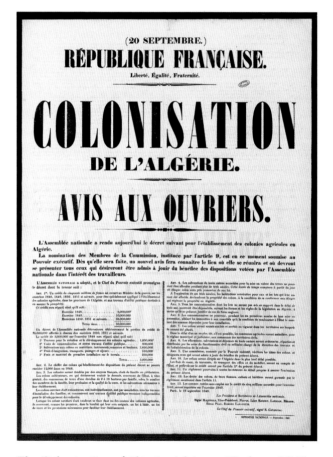

The Colonization of Algeria, Advice to Workers, 1848.

A territory so large and beautiful would warrant trips and excursions. Here, it's necessary to recall that the country's borders to the west and east weren't set down before 1852 and that those in the south were established even later. After 1900. And while it was tirelessly repeated that the country was huge, empty, and uninhabited, during the entire colonial era, censuses were the object (with good reason) of incessant projects. The conquest of the territory was also justified by a demographic argument that was difficult to oppose. It was thought that the territory was limitless. Africa hadn't yet entirely fallen into the hands of the colonial scissors. It was written time and again that only a few thousand people lived in Algeria on the dawn of the military expedition. But whoever dug into the demographic facts saw these figures fall into doubt. For some, it was about size. It's easier to call for the occupation of a territory if it's seen as vast and "empty." A Native American proverb says, "We destroy that which we don't see." French historians of Algeria point to the collapse of what they stereotypically refer to as the "indigenous" people in the years that followed colonization. For many years, resistance only led to military conflicts, death, repression, sequestration, relegation, and deportation. But, to an even greater degree, it was the poor, the poorest, who found themselves stripped of communal fields, without food, cast into indigence, who died en masse. Cholera and typhus epidemics would wipe out the most vulnerable.

In 1871, with Alsace and Lorraine lost, it was necessary to find a place for their displaced populations. It was said that Algeria's northern zone, from the coast to the Tell Plateau, had been brought under French control. The economy could finally grow. The military, which had set in place the Arab Bureaux,[2] would prepare the land for thoroughgoing colonization. Relocated populations would develop. Military conflicts during the conquest of

Algeria wouldn't stop the development of tourism there. The first travel guides date from 1836. Then in 1862, the *Guide Joanne* (the forerunner of the *Guide Bleu*) published its first guide for Algeria, which would be republished more than fifteen times. Its author, Louis Piesse, who had been an important librarian at the National Library of Algeria, would write numerous guides and other books on Algeria and Tunisia. He also wrote an article entitled "The Arab Woman," which appeared in the *Revue de l'Afrique française et des antiquités africaines* (*Review of French Africa and African Antiquities*) in 1887. He writes, "According to God, the master of the world, a girl is worth the same as a boy. That's what Arabs say, but it's different in practice. Because the boy stays with his family, he adds strength to the tribe as one of its warriors. He adds to their fortune and honor while fighting. [...] The girl will add strength to other tribes, to which her children belong." We don't need to spend too much time on these clichés. We must state simply that all of this bad thinking would make its mark, and that today we all live under its influence.

Tourist Algeria was at first a prime spot for hunting. In the nineteenth century, everything was shot, down to the last lion. Then the last ostrich. The Atlas mountain bear disappeared at the same time. Wildlife, virgin land, an Africa so close and so well administered, couldn't help but attract all of the Tartarins of Tarascon, a character so dear to Alphonse Daudet, who followed Chapatin, the lion-killer in his novel of 1863. With the disappearance of the wilderness, it was customary to take pilgrimages into the mountains. Roads and railroad tracks were laid, carrying people to sumptuous destinations, leading each and every person to unthinkably beautiful views. Nothing would be too beautiful for the European tourist.

I was eighteen when I returned to Algeria for the first time. It was the summer of 1981. I was there for several days on vacation. We weren't far from Algiers. In Kabylia. Tigzirt-sur-Mer. The cape in Tigzirt is noted for a high red cliff, on which there remains an ancient site, the ruins of a Roman basilica overlooking a long beach in a cove set back from the open sea. For many years, this amazing beauty was able to hold back the ignominy of the urban ugliness that has now covered over this area. In 1981, the landscape that I saw around me was almost identical to what I had left in 1967. When I was a little girl, my mother would return there in the summer to her parents' home. Here, she would dream, looking out over her family's lands, at the fruit trees that covered the hills sloping down to the sea. This eternal landscape, still the same as it had been in her childhood, this rare and beautiful country formed an amphitheater of breathtaking beauty. It ran from Cape Dellys to the Tizgirt peninsula and its little island, to Cape Tedlès, looking out over the village of Taksebt, with its Roman mausoleum. Modern buildings were few and far between. Antique stelae revealed other names for this Phoenician turned Roman port. Epigraphists discovered the names of Iomnium for Tizgirt and also Ascurus, Ruscurru, and Rusuccuru, for the totality of the site. As for Berbers, they called it Asskour, which is also the word in their language for grace and beauty. When you read works by those who throughout the nineteenth century wanted to take control of Algeria (and conquered lands were seen as propitious for developing new forms of science), it's shocking to witness the manner in which each one cites the necessity of progress and development in an effort to justify his point of view. The logic of science justified all else. A magnificent landscape is described, a land of plenty, with happy inhabitants, abundance, honey and oil flowing ceaselessly, but never in any of these works is any credit given to those who for centuries had shaped the land. These aborigines, these indigenous peoples, these Numidians who had known how to live with Roman civilization, then Christian civilization, then Muslim civilization.

My family tombstones tell a long story. The oldest are undated. On others, it's possible to read 1823–1870, 1839–1865, 1833–1871, 1881–1919. They are there, buried long ago. My mom's house was simple, built up in the hills. Set far from the sea, where the Romans had never built. A long rectangle of precisely quarried stones. Coming perhaps from what remained of a Roman structure. To get there, you must leave behind the immense Mizrana Forest to the west and the ancient city with its basilica and head for the highlands, toward the village of Tifra, which you would come upon as you cross the familial lands of Feraoun. Behind you, to the north, will be Tikobaïn, the hill that leads to the hinterlands and the Djurdjura Mountains. My family was very careful not to ruin the eternal harmony offered by the view of these rare and precious ancient Mediterranean ruins. "Thanks to the indestructible Roman mortar, the walls of the Venice temple were still standing; statues of pagan divinities and proconsuls were sleeping peacefully in the grass," noted Benjamin Gastineau in his 1863 book on lion hunting in Algeria,

> when in 1831, utilitarian engineering, more destructive than the fury of the primitive Christians, of Vandals and Arabs, took these stones, these big lapidarian souvenirs of heroism and ancient beauty, and used them to build caserns, churches, villages, so that we play the drums in a praetorium, we make food before a statue of the Olympian Jupiter cut from freestone, we pray in the temple of victorious Diana. [...] Ancient Rome has not yet disappeared entirely from the land of Africa, where it had once held dominion. [...] Tebessa, ancient Tebeste, on the Tunisia border, is almost entirely preserved with its aqueducts, its elegant Arch of Carcalla, its admirable Minerva

Temple with the missing door. [...] Before coming to Guelma, I went to the doors of the Roman circus, the most complete that I've seen in Algeria. Almost all the seats are intact, as well as the stairs, the grandstand reserved for the proconsuls and the two holding pens in which the belluaires kept the lions and panthers that would fight the gladiators. The theater was complete; all that was missing in these magnificent ruins were the spectacle and the spectators.

Where is the person who will tell us how these men and women knew how to preserve these sites, and how they lived with them?

"Musée de Cherchell: Fragments" (1856–7) by Félix Jacques Antoine Moulin. COPYRIGHT © BIBLIOTHÈQUE NATIONALE DE FRANCE.

Research photography for the video *Tracing a Territory, 2006.* Courtesy of the artist and kamel mennour, Paris (2006) © Zineb Sedira. All Rights Reserved, ARS, New York / DACS, London 2021.

In 1981, I brought a friend with me when I visited. A red-headed, beautiful, white-skinned friend. I say this because it's important to the story. One evening, as night was falling on the seaside, a police car came toward us and asked my cousins, my friend, and me to leave the area because we couldn't be there alone, two men and two women. Karim told the police officer that we were cousins. Back then, he was twenty, like me. His politeness, his music, his voice, his courtesy, his grace, and more than that the promise of life that he carried in himself, were all snuffed out in Algeria. Today, he lives in Berlin. But then, in that moment, the man in uniform turned his flashlight on my friend and, looking at Karim, he said in a tone of disbelief, "Her? Your cousin!" It wasn't unusual to see strawberry blonde hair, hazel eyes, and freckles in that seaside town. But my friend was obviously not from there. But so what? Why didn't the man in uniform look at me? Why didn't he point me out, like he did her? Wasn't I, like her, a foreigner? Was I from there, that country? We were on the beach, with our backs turned to the little hill on top of which rested our house. On the boulders above us, and around the bay, young Algerian men managed their sensuality and their misery as best they could. Under the blankets used as sunshades during the day and in bedrooms at night, the boys lived their lives. There wasn't a single girl to be seen. We had just crossed through the garden, descended the little hill that led to the beach, then the sea. I've never been able to find this little paradise again. I was back in my country for the first time. Where I had been born. That night, in the insouciance of youth and brotherly love, inspired by rock music, which gave us the feeling of community and togetherness, and the pleasure that the water and the sun sent rippling over our bodies, that night, we wanted to take a late swim. Other police officers gathered around. A military car arrived at the beach. All the sounds coming from the boulders stopped. The boys, who had disappeared behind the sunshades, no longer sang. The police officers stood in front of the four of us. Seated, we looked at them; they stood there like immense black trees, masking the last rays of the setting sun. Karim held his guitar on top of his crossed legs. We had left our clothes and our towels up in the house. Night was coming on, and they had seen us swimming from the distance. Our bathing suits were still wet, and they asked us to leave the beach. To go home. The military vehicle came nearer. They said to us, "If you don't leave, it's the police station for you." We didn't resist. What happened in that moment changed my life. I understood that

Algeria, which for so long had remained within the realm of the possible for me, a land of memories and dreams for the future, a country held in reserve, would never be mine.

Back in France, I was overwhelmed by my emotions. I didn't know whether at that moment in Algeria a way of life was disappearing (which for some had never been theirs), or whether everyone was living through the prologue of the decade to come, which would endlessly forestall the promise of freedom so long awaited and so dear to the Algerian people. We know about the violence that was to come. Words, like images, fail us. In 2005, the Algerian artist Zineb Sedira shot a short experimental film in Super 8, one long tracking shot documenting the murderous

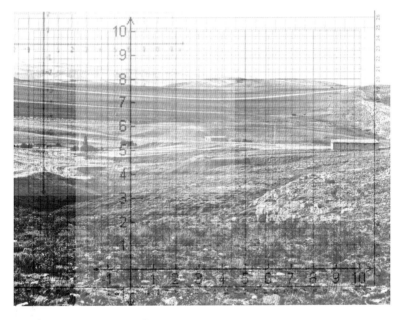

Research photography for the video project *Inconsistent Mapping, 2006*. Courtesy of the artist and kamel mennour, Paris (2006) © Zineb Sedira. All Rights Reserved, ARS, New York / DACS, London 2021.

coastal highway of Algeria and its ghosts. So, life was returning. New artistic vocations were emerging. Often, there is something unexpected about contemporary Algeria. Who would have been able to foresee, not so long ago, the aesthetic force of the new Algerian cinema of today? And, still, like a phoenix rising from the ashes, led by an uncommon generation, the art of Algerian cinema gives us reason to think that beyond the horror and destruction, the desire to record the real can never be extinguished. What else can we say about Tariq Teguia's film *Inland*, other than it's sublime?

Over our several days in Tigzirt, we lived in the house above the sea. We called it the "little cabin." It was on a dune. There, well before independence, French families had built small vacation homes. The "little cabin" was one. To its left was the destroyed chain-link fence of the village health clinic. A little health clinic that survived for the spectacular view that it offered its handful of patients. The vestiges of a singular vacation spot that, in any case, no one can enjoy now.

Many years after this trip, I met a retired man from Lille who asked me, with his eyes red from crying, if it was still as beautiful as it had once been. A soldier, he had been nursed to health there in 1961. I promised that I would send him a photograph of the spot. In 2011, I sent him an old postcard.

The Russian poet Osip Mandelstam wrote about the historical context in which Darwinism was born, when "a stationary natural world ceded place to a living chain of organic beings." It was a vision that Darwin owed to the literary style of Dickens, Mandelstam writes, in which "artistic elements work without cease for the good of scientific theories." While it was true that during the time that Algeria was being colonized writers and painters had the power to influence science, nevertheless it was military men who set the stage for the writers and artists. Writers and artists were indebted to them. Just like the men of science who would follow and who would be called on to describe Algeria. The influence of the military is the missing stepping-stone in the Orientalist argument of Edward Said. The military officers wanted this country. Aristocratic sons and descendants of kings played a major, fundamental role there. Artists would hold steady to this course. This is not the place to discuss their reasons. Perhaps it's difficult to imagine that artists are like military officers. But, in the case of Algeria, it's impossible to say that they were not.

Postscript

My mother never wanted to learn how to read or write. Before her death, when my eldest sister questioned my mother's oral stories and dismissed her talent as a storyteller—my eldest sister, who had seen torture upon torture, death upon death, during the Algerian War, and who never raised her voice, and who had started to listen to the sermons and religious bigotry of a dis-embodied, soulless media—my mother said to me, "Your sister is only a rough draft." We inherit that. The possibility of saying that what is written isn't finished.

ENDNOTES

1. Adolphe Hanoteau, *La Kabylie et les coutumes kabyles (Kabylia and Kabyle Customs)*, Paris: A. Challamel, 1893.
2. The Arab Bureaux developed through the military conquest of Algeria and were consecrated as official organs of the French government in 1844. They put in place expansionist colonial prerogatives and fostered the accu-mulation of colonial-scientific "facts" to sponsor the French "civilizing mission" in North Africa.

YOKO OGAWA has written more than twenty works of fiction and nonfiction. Her fiction has appeared in the *New Yorker*, *Zoetrope*, and *A Public Space*. She has received every major Japanese literary prize and was a finalist for the National Book Award in 2019.

STEPHEN SNYDER is Kawashima Professor of Japanese Studies at Middlebury College. He is the author of *Fictions of Desire: Narrative Form in the Novels of Nagai Kaufū* and has translated works by Yoko Ogawa and Kenzaburo Oe, among other writers. His translation of Ogawa's *Memory Police* was a finalist for the National Book Award for Translated Literature and the International Booker Prize.

Chick Truck

YOKO OGAWA

TRANSLATED FROM THE JAPANESE BY
STEPHEN SNYDER

The room the man had recently rented was on the second floor of a house belonging to a widow, aged some seventy years, and her young granddaughter. The location, forty minutes by bicycle from his job in the center of town, was less than convenient, but considering that he had been thrown out of his last apartment after a dispute with the landlord, he was in no position to be picky.

The old house, distinguished by its maroon tiled roof and chimney, sat on a country road that ran through fields and orchards. There were no other lodgers, so the man had the use of the two rooms on the second floor. From the window on the south side of the house, beyond an irrigation ditch, groves of plum trees were visible as far as the eye could see.

The widow, a brusque, ill-mannered woman, worked in a vegetable market managed by the local cooperative. She was somewhat overweight, like a plump child, and constantly short of breath, perhaps the result of a heart condition.

Her new lodger worked as a doorman in the town's lone hotel. For forty years, from the time when he was still a teenager, he had spent his days in the lobby, and now he was approaching the age of retirement. Greeting guests, carrying luggage, directing traffic, vacuuming the carpet, cleaning the glass in the revolving door, hailing taxis, loading bags in the trunk, and bidding guests farewell . . . that was the man's job.

On the whole, he found his new quarters much to his liking. The rooms were bright and airy and more spacious than his previous apartment, and, best of all, the rent was cheap. But there was one thing that worried him a little—the widow's granddaughter. She was a small girl, six years old and on the thin side, with large, dark eyes. She was dressed almost always in a skirt that was a bit too short and white socks. Her long hair fell in braids about her shoulders.

The girl had come to his room for the first time on the day after he moved in, before he had even finished unpacking. His underpants, which had been drying on the windowsill, were blown by the wind into the garden, and she had retrieved them and brought them upstairs.

At first, she had stood in the doorway, looking down at her feet as she folded the briefs in half, and then into a triangle, before unfolding them again. Though she was only a child of six, it made him uncomfortable to watch her fumble with his underwear.

"Why . . . thank you," he said, feeling he had to say something to her.

But no matter how long he waited, there was no reply. The girl merely tucked her chin deeper into her chest and continued to fold and unfold the underpants, faster now than before and with no sign that she had any intention of returning them to him.

He had no idea what to think. Perhaps he had spoken too quietly, or perhaps he, as the new lodger, wasn't to her liking, or perhaps she wanted to keep the briefs.

Children had always been a puzzle to him. He had no younger sister or brother, nor any younger cousins, and he had never

84

been a father. When he had first come to work at the hotel, he'd received some training in the proper way to deal with small children, but the lessons had been conducted using dolls and dummies.

"I'm sorry you had to come all the way up here," he said.

In response, the girl looked up and stared him in the eyes. He took a step back. The girl folded the briefs still more tightly and gently set them on the edge of the bed.

"I'm going to be living here now," the man said. "I'm sure we'll be good friends."

He spoke formally in the tone he'd learned as a doorman, determined to show her his best manners. But the girl said nothing and simply slipped past him and ran from the room. The underpants she'd abandoned on the bed were a mass of wrinkles.

When the man finished work, he would return to his room, and before he had even changed his clothes, he would sit and look out of the window. Raising his head and staring into the distance was his way of marking the end of a day he had spent with his head bowed before others. The nature of his work meant that he got home at all hours, sometimes in the afternoon but just as often in the middle of the night. When the widow was home, he could hear her loud voice as she scolded her granddaughter or talked at length with someone on the telephone. Cooking smells rose from the kitchen along with the banging of pots and clattering of dishes. Alone in his room, he imagined the day's menu. Hamburgers, cabbage rolls, an omelet, fried shrimp . . .

Since he ate three meals a day in the employees' cafeteria at the hotel, the widow's kitchen was of no concern to him. Still, he could easily guess from the odors that her food was meticulously prepared and delicious, in contrast with her rough manner. He would rest his elbows on the window frame and one by one review the various insults, complaints, and lectures he had received from the guests and his superiors during the day, while imagining the widow and the girl eating their modest meal right below his feet.

But when he returned late in the evening, after they were already in bed, he would take care to climb the stairs as quietly as he could, and then open the window and stare out into the night. On occasion, he would have a single glass of whiskey. At first, he could see nothing in the darkness, but then gradually, from one corner of his field of vision, the contours of various objects began to appear. A creeping rose climbing the gatepost, a bicycle and tricycle leaning against each other, moonlight glimmering on the surface of the irrigation ditch, the plums in the orchard that seemed a shade darker in the night. As he looked out at these things, he felt the troubles of the day recede, and in their place the world of the night enfolded him in a gentle embrace.

It was about ten days after he had moved to his new room that he first realized that the widow's granddaughter never spoke to anyone.

"I know she doesn't say a word, but don't think it's because I haven't tried to educate her," said the widow as he was oiling his bicycle in the garden. "She used to talk well enough. Like any other child, she started with 'ahh, ahh' and 'wah, wah' when she was a baby and then moved on to 'mama' and 'papa'—even though her 'papa' disappeared soon after she was born and hasn't been seen since. No, actually she was cleverer than other kids. She could read her picture books and sing her nursery rhymes better than most."

Though the man hadn't asked her anything, she rambled on, as if she'd told the story many times in the past.

"But her mother died exactly a year ago, and since the day she came to live with me, she hasn't said a word. I thought there might be something blocking her throat, so I took her to a nose and throat specialist. I even took her to a child psychologist and they did that play therapy. They tried friction massage and shiatsu, acupuncture, urine therapy, fasting—but nothing worked. She started elementary school this year, but that only lasted three days. At this point, I suppose there's nothing to be done until she decides for herself that she wants to talk. You know, I can't remember how her voice sounded anymore."

The widow sighed and looked over at her granddaughter, who sat on a stump on the far side of the farm road. She was using a branch to trace something in the dirt, and it was difficult to tell whether she knew she was the topic of conversation.

"Well then, I'll be expecting the rent soon," the widow added, and, having said what she'd come to say, she went back in the house.

The man went on working for a while on the bicycle. There wasn't much left for him to do, but now that he'd been told about the girl's background, if only in the most general terms, he found himself wondering whether he should ignore her completely or whether that would be terribly impolite . . . and while he wondered he lost his chance to make a graceful escape. Under the clear, cloudless sky, the plum trees were bathed in a blinding light.

At that moment, a small truck came bumping up the road. It clattered wearily along, its wheels catching the ruts and potholes. It emerged from a cloud of dust and sunlight, gradually approaching with a cargo of something soft and fluffy and colorful that had been packed tightly into the back.

The man and the girl stood up at the same time. The brokendown truck made an odd contrast with the load it carried, a mixture of pink and pea green, blue and crimson, all in a wonderful marbled pattern. The pattern seemed to shift from moment to

87

moment, as the colors swirled and squirmed. Then they heard a great chirping, so loud it drowned out the sound of the engine, as the truck passed along the road between the man and the girl.

"Chicks . . .," the man muttered. Probably being taken to sell at a temple fair somewhere. Even after the truck had receded into the distance, the chirping still reached them, borne back by the wind. The girl had climbed onto the stump and stood on her tiptoes, staring up the road. Long after the marbled pattern had shrunk to a single point and vanished altogether, she stayed on the stump, craning her neck, straining to hear.

Around them, silence had returned, the cloud of dust had settled. At last the girl climbed down from the stump, and, just as she did, their eyes met across the road. Once again, the man found himself inexplicably flustered, and he crumpled the oil-stained rag in his hand to cover his embarrassment. As usual, the girl said nothing but continued to hold his gaze.

Those were chicks?

Yes, chicks.

Ah, yes. Chicks.

So it seems.

Definitely chicks.

At that moment, without a single gesture, let alone a word, a rainbow named "chick" seemed to span the road between them. Apparently satisfied, the girl erased the picture she'd drawn in the dirt with the toe of her sneaker, brushed the dust from her skirt, and walked back across the garden. As he watched her go, the man rang the bell on his bicycle, quietly so that he alone could hear.

One day, when the man was returning at dawn from a night shift, he found the girl sitting halfway up the stairs to his room.

He knew that he could expect no answer even if he wished her good morning. He could also see that there was not enough room to slip past her and make his way upstairs. Though if he asked her to move and she ignored him, the situation would get even more complicated. But why was she sitting there in the first place? Could it be that she was waiting for him? No, why would she do that? What business could she have with someone like him?

The man continued to ponder, unsure why he always ended up thinking such useless thoughts when he was in the girl's presence, and it struck him as unfair that she seemed perfectly comfortable with the situation. The morning sun through the skylight fell across her face. The widow had apparently already left for work, and the house was quiet.

Suddenly, the girl held out her hand. Since there were never any words preceding them, all her actions seemed sudden to him. The abandoned shell of a cicada rested on her palm.

Yes, no mistake about it. A cicada shell. The man squinted at the tiny object. But if he was being asked to understand something from the shell, he was at a loss to know what it was. Perhaps it was some kind of seasonal greeting, her way of saying that the time had come for the cicadas to begin their droning. But do children know about such things? Or perhaps she was boasting, letting him know that she had found the first shell of the season. Or perhaps she simply wanted to shock him. Perhaps it was her little scheme to spring something ugly on an adult, just to tease him. But if that was the idea, it was already too late to play along—he hadn't shown the least surprise.

When he looked again, the man could see that her hand was very small indeed. Smaller than anything he had ever encountered. Her palm was barely large enough to hold the cicada shell, and her fingers were so tiny that he wondered whether they could possibly be of any use to her. The nails were almost invisible to his old eyes. Yet oddly enough the hand was shaped exactly like an adult's, the joints moved in the same way, it had the same fingerprints, the same patterns on the palm.

As he studied the hand, he came to realize that the cicada shell was not simply a greeting, nor was it a threat. Tension filled the palm she extended toward him, with every nerve focused on avoiding damage to the tiniest leg on the shell. Her lips were pressed tightly together to keep her breath from blowing it away. For the girl, the shell was something precious.

She held it out to him.

"For me?"

The girl nodded. As carefully as he could, the man took the shell from her hand. It was so impossibly light that he almost imagined he had taken her fingers by mistake. Before he could thank her, she ran down the stairs.

The man put the shell on the windowsill, looked at it for a while, and then crawled into bed and slept.

The moments just before dawn were his favorite time to sit by the window. The darkness began to dissolve in the east, as hints of light tinted the sky. The stars blinked out one by one, the moon faded. But despite the world undergoing these enormous transformations, there was no sound at all. All of this change occurred in complete silence.

The man set the cicada shell in the palm of his hand, just as the girl had done. Looking out at the quiet of the dawn, he asked himself whether this was what was meant by a "present." He tried to remember whether anyone had ever given him a present before. Closing his eyes, he searched his most distant memories, but nothing came to mind.

So, in the end, he had no way of being certain whether the shell was a present. It occurred to him that it would be terrible if he were convinced it was while the girl had not intended it that way, so he decided to do his best not to think about the shell. But every time he went to sit by the window, he found himself resting it on his palm.

At some point, the last stars disappeared and the glow of dawn spread over the sky. A single ray of light found its way into the orchard, then two or three. But the quiet, guarded by the last traces of the night, lay cupped in the man's hand. It would be some time still before the sunlight reached the shell.

After the cicada, the girl brought him the shell of a dragonfly. Then a snail shell, followed by the chrysalis of a bagworm and a crab shell. But the highlight was the skin shed by a rat snake. Fifty centimeters long and two centimeters in diameter, it occupied most of the windowsill. The collection of shells grew day by day.

When the girl contemplated her handiwork, a look of satisfaction spread over her face. The two of them began to spend time together by the window. The girl would sit down in front of her collection, and the man would stand by awkwardly or perhaps bring her a glass of juice.

At first, the man wondered how he could manage to pass the time with someone whose age was so removed from his own and who did not talk, but he got the knack of it soon enough. It seemed, finally, that they would simply stare at the shells. That alone was enough for both of them.

The more the man stared at the shells, the more he learned about them. The molted forms were exquisitely made, from the wrinkles carved in the cicada's abdomen to the fine hairs at the tip of its head, from the dragonfly's transparent eyes to the mesh pattern on its wings. The shells faithfully preserved every detail of the animals that had once lived in them. Though they were destined to be discarded, extraordinary care had been taken with them, down to the tiniest detail. Though they were delicately formed, there were no seams or tears. Other than one opening on the back that seemed almost like a zipper, nothing else was broken or crumpled. The skin of the rat snake had been shed inside out, revealing the intricate pattern on the interior.

It occurred to the man that no human being could shed his clothes as skillfully as these animals, and somehow this miracle made his presents seem all the more valuable.

Still, he never spoke of this to the girl. Not because he knew he'd get no answer, but because it seemed fairer to him if neither of them spoke. Even without words, he understood when they were together that she made the same discoveries he did about the shells.

She would poke at them with her finger, hold them up to the light, sniff them. Then, as she thought for a moment, a smile would come to her lips. Each time she moved, her braids would brush her shoulders. When she had finished examining all the shells, she would return them to their original places, exactly as the man had arranged them on the windowsill.

As he had with the shells, the man continued to make discoveries about the girl. It was not just her hands that were small, it was every part of her body. Her nose and ears and back were all so tiny that it seemed God had taken special care in crafting them. Her hair had a wonderful smell. The black of her pupils was so deep that you might almost forget they were intended for seeing things. The mere thought that he himself might have been like this at six made him inexplicably sad.

"Where are you? Dinner's ready." The widow was calling the girl from the kitchen.

* * *

The girl was in the man's room when the truck full of chicks came by for the second time. When they heard the clattering of the engine, they knew immediately what was approaching. The man opened the window.

Just as before, the back of the truck was filled with the colorful birds, and the same chirping could be heard. The girl's face lit up, and she stood at the window on tiptoes. As she did, her skirt pulled up, and the man worried that her underwear might show. But the girl, completely unconcerned, leaned out over the windowsill, straining to be even the tiniest bit nearer the chicks. Fearing she might fall, he took hold of the suspenders holding up the skirt.

Chicks, yes.

That's right, chicks.

This second time, it took only a brief glance between them to confirm their discovery. The girl gripped the windowsill and stared out without so much as blinking, as if unwilling to risk missing a single moment. In the familiar scene outside the window, only the contents of the truck were extraordinary. The feathers bathed in sunlight were a garden of flowers, the chirping a joyful chorus.

But the man knew. The colorful chicks were not long for this world. In the press of the crowd at the temple market, illuminated by a warming light, they would be stuffed into little boxes. Grabbed by the neck, pulled by the feet. But once they were brought home, their owners would soon lose interest, the feathers would fade, and they would sicken and die, covered in their own droppings. Or be eaten by cats. Those that were not sold at the market would suffocate in their crates.

At that moment, for the first time, the man was glad that the girl did not talk. If she had asked him where the chicks were going, he would not have known how to answer. Should he tell the truth? Lie to her? He'd have no idea.

But since they did not talk, in the girl's black pupils the chicks could go anywhere. They could live happily ever after, flapping their beautiful feathers in a paradise at the end of the rainbow.

The girl found an egg to add to their collection. When she came climbing up to his room with the egg and a sewing box, he had trouble understanding what she wanted to do. At first, he thought she wanted to hatch it to get a chick. But then she took a needle from the box and pretended to be pricking the egg.

Ahh, she wanted to poke a hole in the shell and empty out the contents. Of course, the egg had the most perfect shell of all.

He set right to work. Up until this point, everything in the collection was something the girl had found somewhere or other. But this time they were working together, and he was to play an important part. He would put everything he could into making a shell that would be as good as the cicada's or the dragonfly's.

He inserted the needle in one end of the egg, taking care to make the hole as inconspicuous as possible, and then he put his lips to the opening. The girl sat on the edge of the bed and watched him intently. In fact, the man was not particularly fond of raw egg, but with the girl looking at him with such hopeful eyes, he couldn't allow himself to grimace. Okay, okay. Leave it to me, his attitude seemed to say.

Before long, the slimy, smelly liquid came trickling down his throat. The shell was cold and rough against his lips. Suppressing his nausea, he sucked down the egg before he had time to taste it, his breath escaping from the space between the shell, and his lips making a strange sound.

Gradually, he began to feel that he was inhaling one of the chicks that had died at the temple fair. Mourning a chick that had been dyed a bright color, stuffed into a box, and shipped a long distance, only to die all alone. He was burying the chick in a flower garden, making sure the girl did not notice.

He closed his eyes and sucked out the last drops of liquid. Perched on the edge of the bed, the girl swung her legs and clapped her hands. A small, white shell remained between them. The man added it to the collection on the windowsill, and the egg fit in with the other shells. The girl's applause grew louder.

The man continued to occupy his post in the lobby of the hotel just as he always had. He rode his bicycle for forty minutes, changed into his uniform in the locker room, and stood in front of the revolving door. When a taxi pulled up, he would take the luggage from the guest and ask whether they would be staying the night at the hotel. As he was showing them the way to the front desk, the next guest would already be arriving. All day long, he did nothing but go from the entrance to the lobby and back again. No one looked him in the face, and no one knew his name. On the rare occasion that a guest would thank him, he found himself wondering what he had done to deserve their gratitude.

The other doormen were all much younger than the man. They were stronger and more handsome, and their uniforms suited them better. When they were together in the employees' cafeteria or the locker room, they never included him in their conversation. The only time they spoke to him was when they wanted to trade shifts.

But one thing had changed since he'd moved to his new lodgings. As soon as guests showed up with a child, he began making comparisons to the girl. This one is more or less the same age.

No, she's holding a teddy bear, so she must be younger. That one's running in the lobby. That will never do. Even a child should know better. The girl would no doubt be able to sit on the sofa, straight-backed and quite still, for many minutes at a time. And what about this child? More or less the same height and weight, but her face is completely different. The girl is much prettier. . . . He went on this way all day long.

The man never found it strange that the girl collected shells. They seemed to suit her much better than stuffed animals. Tears came to his eyes and he would struggle to maintain his composure whenever he remembered how she looked when she was searching for shells in the orchard or along the irrigation ditch. Working all alone, she would push through the grass or shake the tree branches or dig in the mud. Her white socks got dirty, her braids threatened to come undone, but eventually she would discover a shell. A cast-off shape that had until recently been occupied by a living creature but was now just an empty form filled with silence. She would gather it up, cradle it gently in her palm, and run to bring it to the man.

By the third time, the girl knew enough about the truck full of chicks to recognize the sound of the engine well before it appeared. She went running down the stairs, and the man ran after her. Standing on the tree stump, she waited, every nerve straining.

Nor was she disappointed. The truck came toward them from out of the distance, trundling along the straight road.

There it is. I was right.

Her face shone with pride.

Yes, you were right.

The man nodded.

Illuminated by the sun shining from behind, the truck glowed with the brilliant feathers of the chicks, packed tightly into the bed in back. So tightly it was impossible to imagine the space could hold even one more chick.

To the man's eyes, the truck seemed to be tottering along more slowly than on the previous occasions. Each time it wobbled or swayed, the chirping seemed to grow shriller, swelling like a wave and echoing far into the distance. The girl was jumping up and down on top of her stump.

Perhaps it's moving so slowly in order to give us a better view of the chicks. Just as this thought occurred to the man, the truck passed by them, veered off the road, drove into the grass, slammed into a plane tree, and tipped on its side. It was all over before he'd even had time to cry out.

The man ran over to the truck. The driver was able to crawl out by himself. Blood was flowing from his forehead, but he seemed to be alert enough.

"Are you alright? Hang on! We'll get an ambulance!" the man said, calling toward the house to alert the widow. He took a towel that was hanging around the driver's neck and pressed it to the wound, while using his other hand to rub the man's shoulders.

At that moment he thought to look up—and saw nothing but chicks filling his field of vision. Expelled suddenly from the back of the truck, they were agitated, confused, panicky. One group was twirling about for no apparent reason, another group was flapping their useless immature wings as if attempting to fly away, and still another was huddled together trembling.

The girl stood in the midst of all this.

"No, not over there!" said the girl. "The cars will run over you! Yes, that's right, come here, under this tree. Don't be frightened.

You'll be okay, someone will be here soon to help. There's nothing to worry about."

She was gathering them, reassuring them, clutching the most frightened to her chest to warm them. Brightly colored feathers wafted around her.

At that moment the man realized that this was the girl's true present to him. The gift of her voice. An irreplaceable present that had been given to him alone.

His ears recalled the sound of her voice again and again. It would echo forever in his heart, uninterrupted by the chirping of the chicks.

ALEJANDRO ZAMBRA was born in Santiago, Chile. The author of eight books including *Multiple Choice* and *My Documents*, his stories have been published in the *New Yorker*, *Harper's*, *Tin House*, and the *New York Times Magazine*, among others. The winner of numerous literary prizes, including an English PEN Award and a Prince Claus Award, he has also been a finalist for the Frank O'Connor International Short Story Award, the IMPAC Dublin Literary Award, and the Prix Médicis. He was named one of *Granta's* Best Young Spanish-Language Novelists in 2010. His new novel is forthcoming from Viking in 2022.

MEGAN McDOWELL is an award-winning translator who has translated many of the most important Latin American writers working today, including Samanta Schweblin, Alejandro Zambra, Mariana Enriquez, and Lina Meruane. She is from Kentucky and lives in Santiago, Chile.

Library or Life

ALEJANDRO ZAMBRA

TRANSLATED FROM THE SPANISH BY
MEGAN McDOWELL

1

"My nation is my son and my library," Roberto Bolaño once said. I would like to say exactly the same thing, but I no longer have a library—I gave it away. Three years ago, not long before I moved to Mexico, I decided to donate all my books to the university where I worked. If a library is a nation, I sometimes think, melodramatically, I renounced them both.

The desire to possess seems like an incontrovertible force, but even so, reasons abound for getting rid of a personal library: lack of space, moving house, a philanthropic urge, nearness to death, for example, in addition to other reasons that are less precise and perhaps even unknown to the library's owner, such as burnout, depression, or stupidity.

In my case, all of these motivations got combined and confused: the library I had lugged around and protected since adolescence suddenly became for me a kind of cemetery, and none of the usual excuses to justify the accumulation of books— professional or emotional needs, being a collector or a hoarder, etcetera—were powerful enough to free me from that feeling.

In reality, the lack of space argument never carried much weight. At first, the absence of appropriate shelving led to a landscape of towers on the verge of collapse. Later on there was more room, maybe too much: my house wasn't big for a family, but when that family stopped existing, the place became immense for me and my dog Sardina and my cat Oscuridad, and even for the friends who also ended up separated and traded off the guest room. The library kept growing at the speed of a tropical climbing vine, though there was still enough room on the main wall to hang, for example, a beautiful photo of the poet Jorge Teillier that I'd received as a gift from the photographer Miguel Sayago.

The only time I ever counted my books I had ninety-two, all of which I'd read, and a good many I'd reread. Twenty years later and in the imminence of a farewell, it didn't even occur to me to count them, but then I received an Excel table of the inventory that had been patiently undertaken by university librarians: 3,634 books. So, between my twenty-first and forty-first years, I accumulated 3,542 books, or, to put it in more intelligible figures, in twenty years my library multiplied by 39.5. Another way to process the data, maybe the one that most impresses me: during those two decades, another book reached my shelves every 2.06 days.

It's in terribly bad taste to brag about material goods even if the goods in question are books, but I suppose that if it's done in retrospect and from a fairly Franciscan present, the offense is mitigated. Sometimes I catch myself gazing stupidly at that little Excel file, for all the world like a ruined businessman melancholically reviewing old bank statements. The degree of my regret varies: there are days when the memory of those lost books makes me proud, and, indulgently, I even ponder my presumed generosity, or picture some dear ex-students happily perusing my old books in the library stacks. But it also happens that I simply do not know the person who made that decision, as splendid as it was idiotic. I miss certain books in particular and I miss all of them in general, including the many that I never read or I know I never would have reread.

To be sure, while I was speculating about the idea of unburdening myself of my library, I went on accumulating books, which is not so strange, as we smokers know—we tend to smoke even more eagerly when we're talking about the urgent project of quitting.

2

Long before I got rid of my library, one morning in early 2016 and midway through the period I spent in New York, my friend Blanca called me from Santiago to tell me she was pregnant. After the usual questions and congratulations we ended up talking about baby carriages, a matter about which I knew nothing and she and Daniel—the future father—seemed to know everything: they had scrupulously studied all possibilities until they found the ideal carriage, but they were hesitant to buy it, because in Chile it cost nearly double the price in the United States.

In a fit of generosity I would regret for a long time, I offered to bring them the stroller myself when I returned to Santiago. Blanca refused outright, though I heard the hopefulness in her voice (now I think maybe she was doing it on purpose—she *is* an actress). It wasn't hard for me to convince her (or for her to make me believe I had convinced her): they bought the magnificent stroller that very night, and I didn't realize what a mess I'd gotten myself into until a week later, when some long-suffering gentleman from Amazon deposited two enormous boxes in my living room.

Of course, I couldn't turn up at the airport with those boxes—I'd have to put the carriage together and check it as another piece of luggage. I let a few days go by until my friend Rodrigo came to visit from Chile; with that incomprehensible passion some people feel for the unpacking and assembly of apparatuses, he dedicated his first afternoon in New York to putting the stroller together, and from then on it sat in a corner, patiently awaiting the trip.

"*Y el bebé?*" a Colombian employee of Latam Airlines asked me, months later. Her tone was merely curious, but I still got nervous.

"The baby's traveling with his mother," I answered, dignified.

"*Y es juicioso?*"

"Sure . . ." I told her, though I had no idea what she was asking me—at the time, I was unaware of that odd Colombian way of asking if a kid was well-behaved.

"And why don't you travel together?"

"Because we don't want Jacinto"—the name that occurred to me—"to lose both his parents at the same time. They left on yesterday's flight."

I set out for the gate thinking about parents flying to meet up with their children, and I mourned a long series of horrible imaginary accidents. I tried to sleep on the plane, but my somber mood led to thoughts of my dog, who had just died at ten years old: the friend who was house-sitting had spent some awful weeks going back and forth between house and vet. Sardina was an overgrown and good-natured mutt who thanked you for every morning walk with an odd pant of happy exhaustion.

"*Y la guagua?*" the taxi driver asked me hours later, in Santiago.

"There is no baby," I answered curtly.

The man looked at me as though in apology, though his question had been relevant, since we had just loaded in three hefty suitcases and the still brand-new stroller that—thanks to obsessive training on the eve of my trip—I now handled with skill, as if I were a father who was used to putting it together and taking it apart periodically.

The first thing I did when I got home was hug Oscuridad. I expected her to resist, to punish me for a few days, but she accepted me naturally, as if I'd never left. Then I registered Sardina's absence—the too-silent yard, her bowls piled beside a nearly full bag of Eukanuba—and drank a horrible coffee in the living room while I stood looking at the bookshelves. I had almost made the decision to get rid of the library, and if I still had any doubts, they dissipated at that moment: I felt like those books didn't belong to me, that the only things of mine in that house were my cat and my suitcases and that baby stroller that was not mine.

The following week, we went to the veterinarian. I thought it was a routine visit, since Oscuridad seemed bursting with health, but it wasn't—quite the contrary: she died a few days later. After burying her in the yard and crying scandalously for a couple of hours, I started boxing up my books as if they had been hers. It was actually quite reasonable, because over the course of ten years—the same ten my dog had lived: they were never friends, but sometimes they lounged in the sun together—Oscuridad had slept in almost every corner of the library, and had once even defended it from another cat who, like a thuggish kind of literary critic, used to sneak into the house with the sole purpose of pissing on some books.

3

We'd been living in Mexico City for a few weeks when we found out about the pregnancy. Convinced that a father should at least project the illusion of knowing all, during the first months I set out on frenetic walks around the neighborhood to memorize the names of the streets, and I also studied, with a tremendously false calm, the names of trees and plants and birds.

105

At night I focused on the search for the perfect *carriola* (I'm switching to the Mexican word for stroller, because paternity has unfolded, for me, exclusively in Mexican Spanish). Sometimes I spent up to two hours in front of the screen combing the market: I compared models, read reviews, watched enthusiastic and probably false testimonials on YouTube. Blanca and Daniel's carriola was, naturally, on my short list, but I also entertained models that were more portable and thus more compatible with eventual trips to Chile, which in my imagination would be numerous.

So much window shopping was, unfortunately, unproductive, because one afternoon an aunt of my wife's brought us a carriola as a present. The model wasn't even on my ranking. I thanked her through clenched teeth.

4

I had already weathered two earthquakes in my life, but I was absolutely unprepared to face one in this city that not even the *chilangos* who were born here know well. I was looking for the stability of names and the security of maps and I found, instead, an inventory of destroyed buildings that there was no need to study because it imposed itself on its own, with the habitual eloquence of disaster. The earthquake, however, had the strange effect of making me feel simultaneously more Mexican and more Chilean. The day my son was born—I can't help but make this implied phrase explicit: the happiest day of my life—I felt like I'd spent years in this house, that somehow I had always been here, and this evasive, chaotic, inaccessible city, so plagued with contradictions, belonged to me.

During the first outings as the gift horse's driver, I wanted to convince myself the carriola wasn't so bad, but the truth is it was terrible: it was heavier than an anvil, it was hard to turn, and on the way up a hill you couldn't help but think of poor Sisyphus. Though I tried to make fun of my pretensions, whenever I ran across some particularly desirable model, I caught myself fighting back envy. I don't know anything about cars, I'm blind to their presumed beauty, but I guess my jealously was similar to what a minivan driver feels when he passes the kind of splashy cars that successful soccer players or bloodsucking executives drive. Finally, one night my wife complained bitterly about the carriola, and I guided the conversation to create the feeling that the idea of buying another one was entirely hers.

We always used to see a bubble vendor in Bosque de Chapultepec who transported his merchandise in a worn-out stroller, so we gave him ours. He accepted it gratefully, though I had the feeling he wasn't all that impressed by it either.

5

When people ask if I like living in Mexico City I give a resounding and euphoric yes, but really I'm replying to a different question: I very much like our life here, I adore the meticulous challenge of happiness, I love to share my son's joy when he learns words that are new to me—*ahuehuete, chimeco, chirundo*—or he comes out with phrases like *adiós amigo quesadilla*, or plays "duck duck *oca*." I didn't come to this country in search of Pedro Páramo, but I became a father here and now I can't separate the two experiences. Looking at the city objectively would now be, for me, almost impossible; it would be like looking at my son objectively.

When people ask if I miss Chile I give a monosyllabic answer followed by an uncontrolled torrent of confused phrases. Sometimes I say no, and it's a lie: what I mean is that in Mexico City I found sudden roots and the undeserved prize of starting over, and

I find it hard to imagine us being transplanted to Chile. But most of the time I reply that yes, I do miss Chile, that I'm in dialogue with Chile almost all day long and I would never want to conceive of my country as a place that is distant or lost or imaginary. Because I'm aware of those dangers. I think of my Chilean language stopped in time, blended, pushed aside; I think of the vertiginous and explosive problem of finding words of one's own. I think of exiles and migrants as if I could better understand their lives. It's a false feeling, because of course I am not an exile, and though I am technically a migrant with his papers in order, I didn't come to Mexico in search of better luck, but because I fell in love with a Mexican and we decided to live here and have our son here.

During much of the year, the time difference between Chile and Mexico is three hours, which gives me an everyday sense of tardiness; I get up very early, but in Chile it's already eighty-thirty or nine. The radio app lets you rewind the programs, so I rewind to synchronize my two countries. It's a modest miracle—the true miracle would be an app that let you move forward in time—that grants me a certain serenity, as if it were normal to listen to urgent news with a three-hour delay. Moreover, listening to Chilean news has been part of my son's daily routine since the first days of his life. While his mother lies in bed and tries to construct the feeling that she has slept well, we, in the living room, salute the sun and the portrait of Jorge Teillier (which I did bring with me from Chile) and a fluctuating cast of stuffed animals, and we read the book of the moment five or six times (he is currently an absolute fan of *Paco y el rock* by Magali Le Huche: the first thing he said this morning was, in fact, "rock!"). And as we do all of this, the Chilean news of the immediate past plays in the background. Then come a few minutes of independence: he goes to the shelves and handles the books, which in his hands become gigantic Legos, and he brings some of them to me with a smile, as if recommending them. The shelves he can reach correspond to the letters R and S of the English-language books: a lot of Salman Rushdie, David Sedaris, Rebecca Solnit, and Susan Sontag.

As you can see, I once again live in a library, my wife's library, that in certain segments looks a lot like the one I used to have, although instead of growing up with translations, she's read English-language originals since she was little, so that sometimes, looking at the shelves, I have the impression that this is the original version of my old subtitled library. I like to look at the shelves, to imagine her reading those books, to find photos and underlined sections, and to learn that she never fell prey, as I did, to *tsundoku*: she never accumulated more books than she could read. Hers is, moreover, an excellent library, except for the absence—which to me is glaring—of Chilean literature.

I always read a lot of Chilean literature, and I can't resign myself to its scarcity. I do everything possible to get my hands on Chilean books, especially those of my friends or semi-friends or acquaintances, my literary family or stepfamily with its cousins twice removed and those numerous grandmothers and uncles and stepfathers and even those occasional enemies with whom in any case I share something, I don't know what: a plan, a desire, a way of dancing. I accumulate some books, really very few and I refuse to count them, but I'm pretty sure I have the best library of Chilean poetry in the neighborhood of San Miguel Chapultepec.

6

I was afraid my son would grow up believing that *chile* was nothing more than the Mexican word for hot pepper, but that hasn't happened. We went to Santiago when he was only seven months old, and after we got back home, whenever we asked him about

109

the trip, he imitated some Chilean chickens that left a vivid impression on him. Then came an unexpected variant on Chileanness, a whole case for the fantastic Doctor Winnicott: instead of asking for the breast with the word *chichi*, as Mexican children do, my son coined the neologism *chichile*.

Now he is a year and a half and he talks all day long and when I ask him what his country is he replies it's Chile, which fills me with a dopey satisfaction. It's possible I've gone overboard in my indoctrination, because when I ask him where we live he also says we live in Chile. And when I put him in his carriola and ask him where we're going, he says, his face full of laughter, that we're going to Chile.

I like that idea: we live in a country called Chile and we're going in the carriola to another country that's also called Chile to meet up with some chickens. The new carriola, by the way, is really good: light, comfortable, and versatile, and it boasts a giant pocket where we can fit, in addition to the diaper bag, a reasonable number of books. Maybe the entirety of my meager collection of Chilean books would fit in that carriola and I could set up a mobile library, except that I no longer want to lend them out or sell them, much less give them away.

After lunch this afternoon, we set out for Chapultepec Park, and when my son fell asleep I stationed the carriola in front of an ahuehuete tree and I sat down in the grass to read those Chilean poets I admire and miss so much. I want to do that every day.

Mexico City, June 2019.

110

ELIZABETH AYRE is a writer based in New York City. She is currently attending the creative writing MFA program at New York University. This is her first publication.

Election Night

ELIZABETH AYRE

I stop by the side of the street on the way to meet Tenzin and text a friend, "Should I make out with my friend's journalism master's student roommate just to like . . . deal?" as a joke.

I pass a man crouched on a tiny concrete stoop looking at a picture of a map colored blue and red and smoking a cigarette. We all keep looking at this little picture of the country with the outlines of the states drawn in, crosshatches for the undecided.

On Instagram I see a picture of an "I voted" sticker that's been photoshopped to say, "I relapsed" instead.

A guy from my class texts me, "Fuck. Bad Feelings." I reply, "Totally, really crazy energy tonight," half an hour later. At midnight he texts, "Yeah, very. I turned to drugs. Losing my mind. We'll debrief."

I spot Tenzin sitting outside of this chocolate fondue restaurant across from her apartment on MacDougal Street that lets us sit outside at their metal tables and chairs and smoke weed and cigarettes and never asks us to leave.

She is with her roommate, the journalism student, and her boyfriend Yifei. The journalism student is wearing one of those masks with the plastic attachment on it for airflow, the ones I've read don't work. When I ask him how it's going he says he's just been uptown near Trump Tower taking pictures of protestors and trying to interview people. He tells me that all the buildings were boarded up.

"Did it look crazy?" I ask, wondering how it felt to walk past all the plywood storefronts and thinking how the city must feel like some sort of rich ghost town.

"Not really, there were only twelve people there. Three Trump supporters from Long Island. A woman dancing in a tutu for Biden. I took a lot of pictures."

He says he deactivated the fingerprint function on his phone so the cops couldn't use it to determine his identity.

It's so cold out. I'm shivering too much, probably because I'm already stoned. Everyone is drinking wine out of white kitchen mugs they've brought down from their apartment. They have the bottle uncorked under the table.

"There are so many Trump supporters on Long Island. When I went out to see my mom I saw all these SUVs with 'Blue Lives Matter' decals on their rear windows and Trump signs on the lawn."

"That's where all the cops live," Yifei says. He's from New Jersey.

Tenzin has pulled up an article about ICE detention centers on her phone that stays illuminated on the metal table.

"It's so terrible," she says, "have you read about this? It's criminal. This country hates immigrants."

This guy who wears an alien decal on his baseball cap and takes the train from Bed-Stuy every day to stand on a stoop near Tenzin's apartment and sell weed walks across the street to talk to us. His pupils are large and he's not wearing a mask or a jacket.

"Did you vote, Tenzin?" he says.

"I'm from Nepal, how can I vote?" Tenzin says. "Where is everybody tonight?" she asks.

"That building over there"—he points across the street—"that empty fucking storefront, the people that own it hired a security guard to stand there all fucking day and keep us from standing in front of the building."

"Pasha said he's started becoming friends with you guys." Tenzin knows all the delivery guys on the street and gets high with them when Yifei's not around. They never wave to her when he's there, but the times when I see her and the two of us are alone, all these guys always offer to smoke weed with us and tell us they've got pills and edibles and different strains of marijuana.

"Can you imagine if the security guard becomes friends with them, and then they have to hire another security guard to stop the last one from standing there with everybody," I say, stoned and taking a drink of wine from Tenzin's stained kitchen mug.

"And then he becomes friends with everybody and then they have to keep on hiring guards over and over again."

Everyone laughs.

"You want to hear some good news," the guy with the alien hat says, "listen to this: Siri, who is winning the U.S. election?"

The phone says Joe Biden. I don't want to have to explain to him the electoral college and how the popular vote doesn't mean anything and how even if Biden wins the general election it won't matter because of the senate. I don't fully understand it myself and feel like one of my sixth-grade students probably ultimately has a better grasp on how democracy functions in the United States than I do.

"That's awesome," I say, "good news. I hope it's Biden."

"Yeah, fuck Trump."

Earlier that day I bummed a cigarette from a guy on the street who I always see smoking on the corner near my apartment. He gave me a French cigarette, I can't remember the brand. It was so much better than an American cigarette. We talked about the election and at one point, after discerning that I had voted for Biden, he said, "Man, I wish it would have been Bloomberg," and I was so shocked I couldn't even respond.

I pour more wine into Tenzin's mug and gulp it down in big sips.

My phone buzzes. My friend Dave has texted me, "Keep up the good work and one day you're going to be like Ruth Bader Ginsburg, we're all going to be like Ruth Bader Ginsburg, dead in the fucking ground." I smile and text him back, "LOL."

I open Twitter and read someone has just posted, "Republicans be like 'keep calm and carry that baby to term you fucking whore.'"

"What time is it, it feels like a million o'clock," Tenzin says.

The guy with the alien hat is talking to Justin, "What's the name of that street in Bushwick? Fuck, I used to live right there. You know man, what's the name of it? The main street."

He's staring at his phone zooming in on a map that's not loading.

"I have so much to do tomorrow," Tenzin says.

She's organizing an art show in Brooklyn. Her work: photographs of walls in her village in Nepal printed on canvas and painted over with streaks of white paint. She explained it to me one time, said the white paint had something to do with liminality.

"I can't believe Chris and Melinda backed out," she says. "I had always wanted to show their work, and now they aren't coming because Melinda is apparently sick. But they could have mailed the art at least, or given me some warning, I hope it's not because I slept with Chris."

I haven't seen Chris since college. He used to date a friend of mine. Both of them were anthropology students. Chris was a grad student who travelled to Peru and read playing cards like tarot in the town square to meet people. He'd written his thesis on some sort of peasant uprising he was involved with, but I can't remember now. I remember his paintings, acid sketches of faces composed of many lines echoing inward like the rings on the inside of a cross section of a tree.

Tenzin shows me the flyer and starts rolling a spliff in her lap. I zoom in on Chris's artist statement: "Christopher makes art to heal the traumatized phantasms of hystery and to alert people about the death of nature inside and out . . . Imagination is not radically distinguished from reality but is instead fundamental to cognition itself. This amounts to a reinvigoration of the senses through the liberation of erotic phantasms from their prison in a cave at the bottom of the ocean (the Unconscious) . . ." It goes on. "Themes include: a deep woods at night, proliferations of spirits, pineal eyes, masks, fetishes, animals, Earth Mothers."

Tenzin lights the spliff and says with blurry eyes, "I'm so happy you are here to smoke this last joint with me. After this we'll stop."

Yifei says, "Yeah sure," and laughs.

"You're quitting Tenz?" the guy with the alien hat says.

"Yeah, we are quitting. I'm going to get toothpicks and fill my pockets with candies. It's just a habit, you know? An oral fixation. You just need to replace one thing with another."

The guy in the alien hat nods. "That makes sense," he says. "Fuck, what was the name of that fucking street?" he asks and points to Justin again, as if he'd know, then turns back to his phone.

"I got my first article published at my internship," Justin says.

"What was it about?" I ask.

"It's about things that you can do after you voted. I wrote a list of ten things to do after you go to the polls. There's this bar on Long Island that will give you a shot of vodka infused with rosemary and lemon and rose hips. It's a little bit more than just a normal shot of vodka."

"That's nice," I say.

"Yeah, it's a real step above what you would normally get."

A homeless man is rifling through trash, opening takeout containers looking for food. He stops and asks me for a cigarette. I give him one.

"Now he's just going to be hanging around us all night," Tenzin says to me under her breath.

"Halsey Street," the hat guy says, "Halsey Street!" He turns to Justin and points and smiles, so relieved by his remembrance, but none of us care.

Someone texts the AA group chat I'm in with these older women from California:

"Guys! I apologize for missing tonight. I came home and tuned in to the boob tube!!! Got sucked in. May the best man win! X"

My old sponsor writes back, "The best 'man' is GOD! Is LOVE! Is TRUTH! Is GOODNESS! We love you Laura ♥"

Tenzin's weed is too strong. I love smoking but my body feels like a frail animal I've been neglecting in my apartment. Yifei and Justin are both staring off down the street. I listen to the sound of the helicopters hovering above monitoring the park for protests.

"I should go home soon," I say, "I'm so cold."

"Do you want more of this?" She hands me the spliff.

"Yeah, sure."

When I stand up to leave I feel so light-headed that I might faint, and stumble while I walk.

We go across the street to Tenzin and Yifei's place and she hugs me goodbye. I think about how we shouldn't be hugging, and how sweet it is that she hugs me anyway.

On the way home I stop by one of the stone benches in the park. There's a large white piece of paper where someone has

written, "Why did you vote?" And left a pen. Below people have
written in the little boxes:

Because I want to kill myself [someone added in different
handwriting: for freedom :)]

Voting is an illusion, nothing will change for dreamers &
immigrants. Fuck Trump.

People died 4 US, We have the right

Because it is my duty

Fuck democracy

It's the right thing to do

Good question!

I vote for Jesus Christ (37:1-13)

Fuck Antifa, Hail Satan

A drawing of a hammer and sickle

For RBG <3

To ensure that there is action against the destruction of the
ENVIRONMENT

To end gun violence

It's the least I could do

I couldn't because I'm a child

Because I LOVE TRUMP

Christians for Trump! Latinos for Trump!

To kindle the final spark

I aint even vote, too many F's, but that shit don't matter.
THEY DON'T CARE WHAT YOU GOT 2 SAY

LOVE for the LGBTQ community

Pro-life #saveourkids

For my 6th grade students, for a president who will unify
not divide us

Human Rights

So I could get laid

Because I care

There didn't seem to be a choice not to

For women's rights and trans rights

I vote for Jesus Christ (Timothy 2:3-5) (Peter 3:8, 9) [some-
one else has written: —> AGREE]

FUCK DONALD TRUMP

The world is on fire. We live in hell. Or is this purgatory?
Every day I wonder if we're even alive.

The Night Train

MARK STRAND

This is the night train to the interior, and that's me

Standing by the window, staring at the ever-deepening dark

Into which the yellow cradle of the moon will rise.

I am in my early twenties, smoking a Kent because

I once saw Richard Wilbur smoke a Kent. The train

Moves by the brown, twisted body of a river,

By rows of trees that shiver as we pass,

By a house with one light burning. And now

The train slows down, nearing a station,

And that's me again, in a long tweed coat

That once belonged to Mr. Wimsatt, leaning

With all my strength into the wind. There is no wind.

KAMEL DAOUD is an Algerian journalist based in Oran, where he writes for the *Quotidien d'Oran*, the third largest French-language Algerian newspaper. He contributes a weekly column to *Le Point*, and his articles have appeared in *Libération*, *Le Monde*, *Courrier International*, and are regularly reprinted around the world. A finalist for the Prix Goncourt, *The Meursault Investigation* won the Prix François Mauriac and the Prix des Cinq Continents de la Francophonie. Rights to the novel have been sold in twenty countries. His latest novel is *Zabor, or The Psalms*.

LINDA COVERDALE has a PhD in French Studies and has translated over eighty books. A Commandeur de l'Ordre des Arts et des Lettres, she has won many prizes, including the International IMPAC Dublin Literary Award and several Scott Moncrieff and French-American Foundation translation prizes. She lives in Brooklyn, NY.

Becoming a White Sheet[1]

KAMEL DAOUD
TRANSLATED FROM THE FRENCH BY
LINDA COVERDALE

That Friday in the summer of 2020, my mother welcomed my brother Fardi once again for coffee. They settled themselves in our sitting room with the big orange mattresses, where a harsh light shining through the curtains tinted the ceiling with nuances and tree leaves caught in a shadow play. Outside the window, the little garden rustled some dwarf trees. Once again Fardi found himself gently remembering his childhood. As for my mother, she was always happy to see her favorite son again after an absence of many years. She would tell him about her day and the day before and even the one before that as she plunged deeper into improbability. And the farther she wandered into the past, the farther away she really went. Joy made her chatty and muddled, and as on every weekend with her favorite son, the familiar silence of the house had vanished. The coffee tasted bad

1. Translator's Note: In standard French, *un drap blanc* (a white sheet) is not necessarily a shroud, but in the Islamic faith, the dead are buried as quickly as possible, the body washed by family members and wrapped in a white sheet. And since this story takes place in Algeria, a French reader will inevitably think of a shroud.

because my mother no longer knew how to prepare it but Fardi listened to her, a little sad, a little distracted, affable in the way a man dying with great dignity can be. He smiled politely and even tried to laugh when she required it. At times, he regretted having shown up to relive this scene, always the same one lately.

For some months, Fardi had often returned on weekends to visit her. Neither of them was amazed any longer by the incongruity of this appointment that was both banal and unimaginable. Her least of all. She never wondered for example how my brother, whom she hadn't seen for years, could in recent months appear every weekend, each time with his hands in his pockets, like someone strolling across the seas separating them as if he were returning from the big city and not faraway Ireland where he had been living for a long time.

Just for the record, my brother Fardi had been given up for dead when he set out for Spain in a longboat of illegal migrants in the summer of 2008. His boat capsized on the high seas and half the passengers drowned. Newspapers and their headlines spread the word. At the time my parents learned something that might be seen as a reason for both hope and despair: half (meaning five) of the illegals had been saved by an English cruise ship and the other five had drowned. So, my parents waited. And my mother almost went crazy and her hair fell out. As for my father, he sank into a kind of indifference that I think was his way of enduring death by imitating it. The main thing is that my brother had been fished out by the cruise tourists, and instead of sailing to Spain, the ship dropped him off in England. From there, fate took a turn toward irony and the north. As the only survivor who spoke English, Fardi was immediately commandeered by the police for their inquiries. Since he had traveled in Libya the previous year, perhaps they suspected him of sympathies or complicities with Islamists. Still, he continued on his way, now as a fugitive, to Ireland where he settled in, had a family, and lived his life. Traveling this long path through death, the sea, and England took him a few years and we had almost no more news from him.

Our family house is in a village not too far from the Mediterranean. Our mother was living there alone after the death of my father four years earlier. Taking turns, I or my sisters would visit to do her shopping, see to her care and personal hygiene, do housework, or spend time talking with her. Always the same ritual. She would endlessly repeat the usual furious complaints about her share of an inheritance stolen by her brothers, her suspicions about the pension my father had left her, voice her contempt for her jealous neighbors or my cousins' ingratitude. We gradually understood that she was losing her memory and sense of reality and sinking into another country all alone, in her own head. Her time was going backwards before our eyes. The malady of forgetfulness was reaching into the very heart of her heart; her body was shrinking and her hands trembled, as vague as a dream. As the weeks went by, and in that extraordinary wealth of details bit by bit imposing its authenticity, my mother described to us, effusively, a thrilling life of honor, daring, and extravagant adventure, played out before the inhabitants of her native village in which she had not set foot, however, for half a century. In this passionate, delirious tale she was spinning for herself, she strove intently, meticulously, to erase my father, the image of my father, all his actions and memories, and even his entire life. So, after a few months, nothing remained of him. And in her triumphant story, after having been a widow, my mother became young again: intrepid, unmarried, a desirable virgin, and then a woman unknown to us all. She went so far back she secured another life that completely escaped us. And in that flight backwards, she became resplendent, and recovered a former beauty. She returned insistently to a particular story, about an imaginary old rifle she used to brandish—she said—at the marriages and harvest festivals of her native village, garbed as a hero whose male family name vaguely recalled, through deformation, her own. She was losing her memory and acquiring audacity. Most astonishing was that forgetting almost everything brought her dazzling happiness. Her face glowed with well-being and peace recovered through obliteration. She was healthier for having renounced all her lived life. Neither we nor the doctors could do a thing about it. Sometimes we laughed at her tales grown powerful, ample, and devastating in their precision. At other times my sisters wept to see her dying, in a way. Listening to them, Fardi would hang his head in distress.

She often spoke of my brother.
     At other times she forgot him.
     About two years ago, whenever she swept the dead leaves in the courtyard, she would announce: "Fardi will return this summer." She would also see him in dreams. And she imagined another life for him, and first names for his unknown daughter. Details of his wife's face. In our old house, this transformation of the present into the past spread to objects and the walls: thenceforth shabby and sterile, the old lemon tree in the courtyard bent down, exaggeratedly heavy, over its own roots as if looking for its shoes to escape from the little garden. Paint flaked to pieces like an ancient lie. Many of our beautiful dishes had broken and all the rooms smelled stale and dusty. My mother lived there but elsewhere, as if retreating backwards towards a birth long ago.

She experienced Fardi's return not as a miracle but as a courtesy, a habit he might have. In her mind, moreover, my brother showed up every single weekend. How? Why bother about that detail. And on that particular Friday in the summer of 2020 (and others thereafter), Fardi kissed her forehead the way we do with our elders in this country devoted to the past (here, in the land of decolonizations, the future is merely a chance to relive the past, cross paths with our ancestors, and go back in time). Fardi drifted towards the kitchen, where he glanced around halfheartedly, making sure the faucets were tightly closed and all food was stowed in the fridge. In the court-yard, with its bare roots of our three trees, the atmosphere of calamity and abandonment that sickened him was confirmed by dead leaves and garbage bins. My mother pursued him, yammering behind his back. "Your aunt has bought a car, a second one for her daughters. The President of the Republic's sister," she added, "came knocking at my door but I refused to open it." Then: "Your cousins want to take our share of your grand-father's legacy." It all came pouring out, endlessly. She wanted to say everything because she was happy.

Little by little, that same story devoured her. The malady became malignant as she accused us, her own children, of forget-ting first names, of not recognizing our dead or remembering her own fake memories! She fabulized, most often about her youth as that brave young man armed with a terrifying rifle and admired for his generosity after the harvest. Fardi tried to resist, in the beginning, with a few replies intended to steer his mother back towards reality, then gave up. Like his sisters. To rise above his sorrow, he often thought about his children and his return trip to Oran, which he envisioned with relief. He too was plunging into his imagination. Sometimes he broke free. As on that Friday (among a hundred others). My mother had fallen silent, as was her wont, in the middle of her story. Then, as often happened, she began to weep, softly, as if to perfect a sweet sorrow, a timid one thus intended to be even more poignant and demanding.

"Why are you crying?" said Fardi, tired of having to ask since he already knew the answer. She turned her head in refusal and he knew that he would have to keep trying to wipe away this routine sorrow. "It's your brother Saad. He is ungrateful and doesn't come to see me anymore." The reproach, voiced at last, came tumbling out. My mother recounted how this eldest son who ought to have taken care of her after her husband's death was avoiding her, stealing her meager savings and leaving her to die of hunger and loneliness. While Fardi searched for something in the black coffee in his cup, my mother painted a portrait of his older brother, Saad, that was harsh and disdainful. "He's selfish and a coward. Do you know that he stripped my house and took all my lovely dishes and antique carpets? He borrowed money from me that he refuses to pay back and he won't help me repair this house I paid for by selling my mother's jewelry." Fardi knew all that and knew that she had made it all up. "He is the eldest but you are the best. I realized that as soon as you were born." Fardi kept listening for a long time. Noise from the cars passing in the lane thinned out his mother's voice and the heavy burden of her accusations. For several months, Saad had almost become her devil. For the past year! He had been guilty of everything. In my mother's eyes, his black portrait combined the features of my father, my uncles, of men who had hurt her, and of others, even more unknown, wandering in her memory in search of a face to acquire. She complained for a long time. The day was waning and Fardi knew he had to drive back to the big city, eighty kilometers away.

Heralded by a jingling bunch of keys, one of my sisters arrived to prepare our mother's dinner. Houria came in and greeted her beloved brother. "How are you, Saad? And the children?" Saad smiled. Losing her memory at top speed, in her retreat this mother was jettisoning her angers as well, taking stock of her hardships, and had fabricated for herself the perfect enemy. She accused me of everything, *me* her eldest son: me, Saad.

When I began undergoing this erasure, head bowed, I did not know what to think. I wasn't angry, or wounded, but intrigued (I'm lying). That was what death was, perhaps: someone speaking to you without seeing you. Or, above all, someone arguing with you while thinking you're someone else, drawing up the list of your vices and virtues. Almost curious (I'm lying when I say curious), I envisaged this beginning of absentmindedness as a chance to experiment with death, but without the grief, or the finality. Or with very little grief. Or just some vanquished and contained grief. Routine is what best imitates death. My mother had killed me and each weekend I die. My duty was to listen to her as a ghost, a revenant she did not recognize. That's how things often go on Fridays: Fardi opens the door, kisses her forehead, and has coffee with her. Whereas I, dead for almost eight years, I watch from behind a parting of high seas.

YASMINE EL RASHIDI is
an Egyptian writer. She is
the author of *The Battle for
Egypt: Dispatches from the
Revolution* and *Chronicle of
a Last Summer: A Novel of
Egypt.* She writes on politics
and culture for the *New York
Review of Books,* and is an
editor of the Middle East arts
and culture journal *Bidoun.*
She lives in Cairo.

Where Are We Now?

YASMINE EL RASHIDI

It was unclear whether or not my brother would leave the house that morning. He slept on the bare, squeaky, hardwood floor of his bedroom, covered by a single bedsheet and with a pillow, for two weeks after we had emptied most everything else out of our home. Around him remained some scattered belongings. A book-sized landscape painting. A set of five hand-painted tiles. His clay bedside lamp, positioned on the floor by the sheet. An eighteenth-century Egyptian tapestry, still hung on the wall. An old wicker chair. And in a corner of the room on a small rug, an assortment of ceramic fragments and pamphlets; presumably things about which he was still undecided. Many of our belongings—a lifetime's worth; seventy-plus years in my mother's case—had been packed and moved around the corner into her new flat. Some things had gone to storage—an antique bedroom set, chandeliers, a billboard-sized oil painting, and a formal dining room that had no place except in the imposing chamber my grandmother had envisioned when she dreamed up the house. The rest went to friends, or people otherwise close to us or in the neighborhood—my father's cook, the building porter next door, an electrician down the street. We made most of the decisions together—my mother, brother, and I—what to keep, what to store, what to give away. Except the selling of the house. That had been my mother's resolve.

The house had taken some six or seven years to come into being in Cairo in the late 1930s. The population was small then, land was in abundance, you could see the Pyramids from most every vantage point. My grandmother, *Granny* to me, dreamt of such a view, and bought the land in 1936—three acres on a residential island in the Nile in the center of the city. She built an art-deco brick and metal fence around it some eighteen months later, and eventually, when she had the money, commissioned the architect. The house would need to be big enough to accommodate the three children she then had, her relatives when they visited from the Delta, and any foreign guests. Then living areas for the house-help, the gardeners, the children's German governess. There was talk that my grandfather's brother, soon to retire from his post as governor of Alexandria, might move in too. He would need privacy, and a place to work.

It all came together just in time for my mother's birth—in the southernmost top-floor bedroom with a corner view to the Nile. The facts are changeable depending on who you ask. My grandmother was in labor for anywhere from one, to three, to five, or fourteen hours. She gave birth either alone or with the help of house staff and her dressmaker. The washerwoman delivered the baby. A doctor may or may not have been present. The rest of the family was gathered downstairs around the living-room fireplace, roasting chestnuts, in anticipation of news. This is the only fact that seems to be held unanimously as truth. Those I asked: my uncle, my mother's elder cousin, my great aunts (the first, second, and third sisters of my grandmother), all before they died.

I could never have imagined that the house would become the central element in my life; like a colonizing force, both anchor and unbearable load—the place I returned to in search of solace, a space I tried in different ways to flee. And how much it had seen by the time I was born into it myself. The fluke of a fourth child born in 1943, ten years after my grandmother thought she would have no more. My grandfather's premature death, his brother's death soon after, the marrying-off of my aunt and uncle as the urgent task of a widow. My mother's willingness to look after her own mother. My father's generosity in accepting to live with his mother-in-law when my parents married in 1973—a proposition unheard of at the time. This was how my brother and I came to be the only grandchildren to grow up in the house, to call it home.

Fast-forward. A population exploding despite a visible birth-control campaign spearheaded by Mrs. Mubarak. The city center now so dense, green space hard to come by. My grandmother's death, my parents' divorce. Three siblings now heirs to the house, along with their spouses and all their children and in some cases grandchildren, vying for their rights. My mother, my brother, and I alone. My mother resolute: There would be no selling of this house, no matter its monetary worth. This is where she would die.

I was seven-turning-eight. I watched from between the banisters, through keyholes, from behind cracks in open doors, as many, and then most of the rooms in the house were closed and locked. In the upstairs hallway between our bedrooms, in a built-in closet camouflaged in the wall, I observed my mother place the keys. In a turquoise pouch with a zipper. Under a set of towels. The key to that closet was in the next one, under the sheets. I understood the gravity of the safeguarding of the house from my mother's posture—the stiffness of her body as she hid the keys away. The tension in her neck. Her general silence.

None of us really slept that night in my mother's new apartment. I got up several times in the dark, disoriented, unsure as to the direction of my bedroom door, taking a moment to register where I was. From her new terrace, I looked across the building's back garden, over the hedge, to our soon-to-be old house. My brother's sheet-side light glowed through the window and haze of his muslin curtains. Through the slits of the French-window shutters leading onto the terrace where I sat, I could see my mother's light on too.

I tried to find meaning in this new setup: The rooms that my mother recreated to mirror as closely as possible those of the house, only compressed into smaller spaces, and pivoted 180 degrees. The view of our house from almost every balcony and window of *the flat*, as I had taken to calling it. The fact that you could only reach the building by car if you drove past the house. There was no other way around it. So we took to walking, in avoidance of the view, but I couldn't help but peek, from windows, behind curtains, checking in on the house, at least several times a day. I wasn't sure what I was looking for exactly. The new owners? Signs of renovation? A ghost? I had always believed the house was possessed, and maybe I was looking for an indication that an ancestor would protect it. In those early days I wasn't entirely sure either from what. Perhaps from a gaudy renovation, or demolition. To this day I'm unsure which of the two is worse.

My brother had watched with an expression of horror as my mother and the new owner signed the legal deed confirming the handover of the house. We sat in the garden, my father there too, on that April morning, the second day of the month, 2018. I recorded it all, with a camera and the audio option on my phone. My brother had carried out the last of his belongings earlier that morning, leaving nothing behind except the mural on his bedroom wall that he had painted over several years in his twenties. There had been talk in the early days of packing of bringing in conservators and removing that too, but somehow it was the one thing that slipped away, undiscussed. We had taken our first family photo in thirty years in the hours before the handover, and reenacted images from childhood. My father, who had held me by a pear-shaped ficus tree when I was six months old, now stood by my side, the tree overgrown and lopsided. My mother beside me some few meters from that spot, replicating a photo in which she's carrying me the day my aunt's husband died, the day Sadat signed the peace treaty with Israel. My brother and I in a corner in the garden, as we were as children, looking up. My mother, by the playhouse, by the front entrance, the back stairs, the rosebush. The four of us together, in the house again, for the first time since my father had left. It was my idea, these photos, an attempt to make more memories in those final hours, after rediscovering and throwing away bags of them as I had sifted through rooms and remembered again. We walked out of the main gate of the garden that day not saying a word, conscious of the new owners and their entourage of lawyers behind us, watching as we crossed the front lawn. My mother walked stridently, looking more determined than I had ever seen her before, intent on masking all emotion. A neighbor sent an SMS. She had been watching from her balcony, observing the shutters of the house as they were closed for the last time.

I wish I had words to evoke how I felt that day, but neither do I know how I felt, nor do I understand what it means that the first thought that comes to me is that I felt nothing. I'm sure I wasn't feeling nothing. I had spent the six months leading up to that moment—starting from the day my mother signed the contract of sale—in what felt like a disembodied state. One day I was in my life as I had always known it to be, at home at my desk entering the house going into the garden going upstairs to the kitchen playing with the dog, and within the space of some few hours of leaving it and coming back again, I no longer knew what I felt. I walked into and through my life as I had known it for the past forty years, everything in place as it had always been, and yet nothing quite the same.

My goddaughter spent half of each week with me during those last six months. She asked questions with persistence. Why didn't my grandmother leave the house just to my mother? Why did my aunt care about money so much? Why didn't my mother just say no? Why didn't she put her foot down? And when she did, what was the response? She sat beside me as I sorted through things, my own as well as my grandmother's, and also things my father, my uncle, others, had left behind. The basement and attic had been like dumping grounds, with cupboards, entire rooms, untouched since my mother had been a child. My goddaughter quickly came to understand that my interjections were signs of memories triggered by *stuff*, and asked for a camera to record her own memories in the house. She was six then but a quick study. I gave her most of what she asked for from what we found of my life. A plastic rabbit that glowed in the dark, a beaded purse, a hard-shell fuchsia handbag, some rubber toys, pens, notebooks, other odds and ends. She took them home to my father—her guardian by way of a long story for another time—and announced to him that she had acquired his daughter's memories.

I regretted not photographing the bric-a-brac cart filled with things that I recognized as mine when I encountered it on the street. I watched it pass me by and regret came over me even before it was too late. I wished I had taken my mountain of garbage bags full of paper—drafts of university essays, early stories, manuscripts, boxes of rejection slips—to the recyclers myself to turn into paper that I could use one day. I wish I could claim to know at least what kind of paper this part of my life was turned into. Where it is. What its new life may be. I regretted the Super 8 film that was used haphazardly, without clear structure or intention. I regretted canceling the documentary about the leaving of the house by my friend Tamer Said. I regretted not starting earlier, to document time, space, sound, light, color. I wished I had been doing it for years, in anticipation of this moment that we must have known would come.

The soundscape of my mother's apartment is almost identical to that of the house. The birds in the mango trees dividing the grounds of the house from the building are the first sounds of the city for us at dawn. On her back balcony, where I've sometimes sat writing late into the night, music from across the Nile still filters through, mimicking what I used to hear on my first floor terrace, where I had presciently scripted into existence through fiction the packing of the house. If you listen closely enough, perhaps on a weekend, if anyone happens to pass by, you can hear the ring of our old garden-gate bell. In early spring, as the sun sets over the Nile, a mercurial coral that turns orange, the light falls into my mother's kitchen, casting color and shadow as it did in the first-floor rooms of our old house that I had claimed as mine.

As I write this, I am in the first days of a move into a place of my own, across the river, in a new neighborhood. Over the year of renovating my apartment, I tried to make the simplest choices I could. Unfinished wood, poured aggregate floors, doors without keys, locks, handles. So far I've unwrapped just some of the artwork that I'll eventually hang, including the framed front page of the newspaper from the day Hosni Mubarak stepped down.

My brother and I are each taking notes on all the mint-green art-deco bathrooms we come across that are near-replicas of the childhood one we shared upstairs in the old house. Together we have collected identical tiles, and plan to reconstruct the bathroom somewhere one day, even though I'm well aware of not wanting to live with that mint green again. The new owners still haven't moved in, puzzling us, but I still take photographs, even though the house looks as it did on the day we left. From behind the main garden gate you can see the sun exposing different rooms upstairs at different times of day—the forest green dining room, my mother's beige living room, the petroleum blue childhood bedroom that was my mother's before it was mine. Although the lights inside remain off, after sunset the street lamps reflect off the windows, illuminating the various shades of colored, fluted glass.

My mother effectively left the house the day her bedroom was moved around the corner. Over the next two weeks, she arranged her new apartment. By the time she signed over the deed and the house was no longer hers, she had made sure every painting was in place and even installed new artwork for the bathrooms. In that way, my mother has faired better than us, quickly calling her new space home. After being harassed by the family heirs for thirty years, she says she feels satisfied that she sold on her own terms; to the buyer of her choosing, at the time that felt right for her. Our entire neighborhood heard the news about the sale, but the greengrocer and supermarket continued to write "the villa" on receipts delivered to the new flat. Although she had always said *the villa* had been her identity, my mother holds herself now with a different kind of confidence, and ease. The apartment she now lives in also belonged to my grandmother—it's part of a three-story building Granny acquired from a Jewish family fleeing Egypt during Nasser's rule. She gave the first floor to my uncle, a garden apartment to my aunt, and had planned for my mother to move into the second floor when she eventually married. In those early days following the revolution of 1956, with the house still full, my grandmother couldn't have imagined that one day her daughter would find herself there completely alone. Knowing my own mother, who is equal parts spiritual and religious, I believe she finds faith in this: the fact that in some sense she has ended up where she was always meant to be.

VALZHYNA MORT is the
author of *Factory of Tears*,
Collected Body, and most
recently, *Music for the Dead
and Resurrected*, which has
been named one of the Best
Poetry Books of 2020 by the
New York Times and NPR
and was shortlisted for the
Griffin Prize. Mort is a recip-
ient of fellowships from the
National Endowment for the
Arts, the Lannan Foundation,
and the Amy Clampitt Fund.
Her work has appeared in
the *New Yorker*, the *New
York Times*, *Best American
Poetry*, *Poetry*, *Granta*, and
Poetry Review, among many
other publications. Born in
Minsk, Belarus, she writes
in English and Belarusian.

Try to Summarize a Mutilated Year

VALZHYNA MORT

I spent 2020 trying to keep track of the arrests of the friends—poets, artists, and journalists—I know and I don't know in Belarus. It was a Brownian motion of detentions, hearings, sentences, diagnoses (Covid-19 was intentionally spread in Belarusian prisons), and releases. Some poets were detained randomly on the street. Others were targeted. Many were detained right at their public performances. Everybody grew paranoid over steps outside their apartment or a van driving by. Poet Dmitry Strotsev had a bag put over his head when he was returning home from running an errand. The policeman who shoved him into a van said: "I hope your heart isn't weak." In jail he met a man who showed him a pillow made out of his daily rations of bread (the prisoners sleep on the floor or a metal cot without any bedding). Poet Uladzimir Liankievič was detained twice. First time, for singing a song ("Why were you singing on the street?" the judge asked. "Because when I sing, I'm less afraid," he responded.) And second time, for just being out on a Sunday, which is the day when Belarusians come out and stroll across their cities: a stroll through a city in the 2020 Belarus became an act open to political and ethical interpretation, with unexpected legal consequences. ("Why were you outside?" the judge asked Uladz as an accusation. "I live here," he answered, and got thirteen more days in jail.)

Following his sixth, so-called re-election, Alyaksandr Lukashenka got so paranoid that he decided to treat every single person as his opponent and therefore, a criminal. (A Belarusian joke: a man who is being detained screams: "But I voted for Lukashenka!" "Liar! Nobody voted for Lukashenka," the policeman screams back.) In just a few months following the elections, tens of thousands of people were detained. Every detention was accompanied by the horror of torture in police custody. Men and women, young and old were beaten—to comas, to seizures, to permanent disabilities, to death—on the streets, inside police vans, in their cells, prison yards, and prison corridors. The legal system was dismantled. No lawyer, no human rights organization could defend your innocence. People were trapped inside their own country at the mercy of a madman and his henchmen. Yet, they kept coming out for weekly strolls, for music and poetry gatherings.

Foreign journalists, expelled from the country, kept asking: "This is not the first rigged Belarusian election. What has changed?" The answer is always the same: photographs of the tortured, mutilated bodies of your people. Grown men undress in front of the camera to show their injuries. They want to give testimony. They talk of standing in the winter cold with their hands up for hours next to a prison wall. They talk of a man pleading "just kill me already" as he is being beaten by police. A man with broken bones on a hospital bed says he ran out to buy baby formula and now he is here, wearing an adult diaper. He feels lucky to be hospitalized from prison. Videos of senseless police violence next to children's playgrounds, next to park benches. Videos of murder. A body of a political prisoner who "died" in

144

custody and is returned to his parents bandaged so that only his mouth is visible.

Once you see your own people as tortured bodies, you will keep seeing them that way for the rest of your life. Their bodies, not the sky, not the streams, will be standing in front of your eyes when your child says: "Name something blue! Name something red!"

Belarusian condition catastrophizes simple narratives and ready-made cliches. In October 2020, writer Alhierd Bakharevich said in an interview: "We have already won, which is why we will be executed." Belarus revealed the vast gap of absurdity and despair between the idea of a broken legal system and a total legal collapse. Belarus is not Stalin's Russia. It is alike and different from other authoritarian regimes. A country held hostage. Hostages on their way to work in the morning. Hostages picking children up from school. Hostages shopping in the grocery stores. Even those who managed to flee remain Belarusian hostages on the streets of Berlin or Warsaw. This is not a revolution that one carries out once. This is a revolutionary change that consists of daily ethical choices, banal, brutal, and hardly visible to the outsiders.

Ministry of Internal Affairs, in Seven Cantos
SIARHIEJ PRYLUCKI

CANTO I

My brother and sister work there,
a jolly uncle, thrice-removed,
Dad used to work there, now retired
but maintains close connections
unlike the connection
with his head and heart.
We live in a building on top of a former graveyard,
buy groceries in the store on top of a former slaughterhouse,
Mom works inside the former insane asylum
as an elementary school teacher.

CANTO II

As long as I remember myself, our family
followed a strict regime:
wake up by the bell, sleep by the bell,
eat on schedule,
a brutal hierarchy of love relations
between those who have birthed us and now
struggle to conceal disappointment.
I was beaten with love,
I was loved in small doses,
my memory is weak and exotic.
In the photographs we are all happy.

CANTO III

My brother works for riot police,
a regional champion,
top military student,
family man, drinks, doesn't smoke, beats his wife,
as is traditional in patriarchal circles,
madly loves children.
Love of children here is nationally acknowledged.
Never talks about what he does at work.

CANTO IV

My older sister is an investigator at a detention center,
a quiet, invisible little woman,
always says her hellos and goodbyes,
never the center of attention,
hasn't married, doesn't harbor any illusions,
gets by on sporadic emotions,
she showed me "cool" photos from interrogations
   —Look this one has peed himself!
   —Check this out, a man weeping, what kind of a man is he now?
I remember how as a child she cried
having run a splinter into her finger.

CANTO V

Maria, 25—
ran out to a store
uterine rupture, multiple hematomas
Aleh, 48—
disorderly conduct
concussion, corneal detachment, amputation of phalanges
Victoria, 41—
came out on a balcony
bullet wound in the stomach
blood gurgles like volcano magma
Nadzeya, 23—
danced in the fountain of a water cannon
her prosecutor is asking for eight years in prison

Andrei, 17—
rectal rupture inflicted during an interrogation
mother had heart attack, fatherless

CANTO VI

Dante, 20—
died on a surgery table,
a tattoo on one shoulder—
ripped out with meat,
a mole on the face—
ripped out with meat,
the case is closed,
the guilty not found.

CANTO VII

I looked for my friend for a long time
he came outside and vanished
for four days not a word
telephone unavailable
parents hysterical
we found him unconscious in the intensive care
craniocerebral injury, broken ribs, spinal bones
something else scary
doctors didn't even bother to count hematomas
I stood over his bed for four days
everything in the world lost sense
tears seemed so miniscule
radio broadcast a program on the national celebration of literature
and poetry

(translated from the Belarusian by Valzhyna Mort)

Observation
DMITRY RUBIN

Other people's graveyards
grow fast

Winter in Belarus
DMITRY RUBIN

1

When snow falls on the ground
in my country,
it falls facedown,
hands behind its back,
teeth knocked out, in the snow.

2

Under my feet
snowflakes scream
They scream
Idiot
They scream
Where are you heading
They scream
Go back
I envy the snowflakes
I cannot scream
I lost my voice
from screaming.

A Lesson in Endurance
JULIA CIMAFIEJEVA

On my back

the cold with its finger
    childishly
        counts
            spinal bones

The cold writes
in cursive
    pressing
a blue pencil
        into the white paper of my skin

It writes
pain rape scream moan

It writes *evil*
death torturer

The paper of my skin endures
the cold's clumsy handwriting

The cold
just started its studies
of words
these are only words

I have to forgive
the incompetence
of the icy fingers

Don't tear, skin!
Don't break, spine!

Allow the cold *be best*

It requires so much practice
So many backs

(translated from the Belarusian by Valzhyna Mort)

Fall 2020
ULADZIMIR LIANKIEVIČ

1

—all night in the yard people were beaten
all night in the yard people were beaten

the dogs barked
the dogs barked

did you hear?

—cool it
you are imagining things
you are imagining things
nobody was beaten
nobody was beaten
you wouldn't have heard
a truncheon hitting the body

soundless is a truncheon

2

on the security guard's cracked iPhone, my trial.
lower yourself into this chair
look the battery is low
so your hearing will be extra quick
do not contradict
it's in your own interest

if the battery dies
you won't hear your sentence
won't know how long
we'll keep you locked up here
you'll lie on the metal cot
and wonder how much longer
you'll be smelling this shit

we are talking literal shit here
composed of the shit of your cellmate from the lower plank bed
your cellmate from the upper plank bed
your own shit
and this guy who came in last night
hasn't shitted yet
so this shit that we breathe in
isn't yet completed
the newcomer will adjust
and the bouquet will be full

—The court is in session. Why did you leave your apartment?

(translated from the Belarusian by Valzhyna Mort)

LINA MERUANE is the award-winning Chilean author of *Nervous System* and *Seeing Red*. She has received grants from the Guggenheim Foundation and the National Endowment for the Arts, and was a DAAD Writer in Residence in Berlin. She teaches at New York University.

MEGAN McDOWELL is an award-winning translator who has translated many of the most important Latin American writers working today, including Samanta Schweblin, Alejandro Zambra, Mariana Enriquez, and Lina Meruane. She is from Kentucky and lives in Santiago, Chile.

Her Skin So Lovely

LINA MERUANE
TRANSLATED FROM THE SPANISH BY
MEGAN McDOWELL

Mom told us not to worry, everything would be fine without Dad. Such a good person, Mom. And so pretty, now that she didn't cry anymore and she'd gone back to using the lotions that softened her skin. She'd let her hair grow out and the black locks cascaded over her bare shoulders. Don't worry, children, Mother won't leave you, Mother will take care of everything. So confident, she was, her steps so light since he'd left. And she said, Mom did, that even though things outside were hard, there would always be a sun on the horizon. And it was true, there was the sun shining against an astonishing blue, see, children?, look at it there, and she'd open the curtains and the windows to let the day enter, the breeze that smelled of spring. We would stick our heads out and distract ourselves looking at the cats on neighboring balconies and the birds chirping out their boldness on the railings, and also at the moles that ventured through the streets down there, below. We had fun counting the bees that hummed in the gardens full of flowers. We never got tired of naming all the species we'd learned from schoolbooks. At nighttime we stayed awake lying in the big bed of Mom without

Dad, with Mom and her dark curls who let us cuddle up and caress her lovely skin. Her warm skin that smelled of milk. In a cooing voice she told us of the fish that were reproducing in the oceans now that there were no ships interrupting their love or spilling oil and polluting the water. Her voice told us of the white swans that now inhabited the deserted cities, have you ever seen such swans, children?, the colossal swans in the Venetian canals? She told us of the Thai elephants and their babies blithely crossing the streets, and of the roaming cows, of the lions asleep atop hot highways, of the goats frolicking in now-deserted theme parks. She lulled us with pumas leaping the fences around houses and marsupials bathing in pools until the rooster crowed us awake again. How pretty your song, rooster, cried Mom, clapping and laughing like another child among us, making us laugh along with her as if her joy were tickling the hungry children we had become.

M om was another person without Dad in the house. Her skin shone now, there were teeth in her smile, there were lips in her face, pink cheeks and eyes where before there had been only tension. Because Dad had complained about everything, blamed her for everything, punched the table when she served her insipid vegetable dinners, accused her of killing us with hunger, him and her very own children. Mom whimpered. Dad howled: there was no excuse, not the shortages or the closing of slaughterhouses or the meatpacking factories shuttered because of the infection that was spreading through towns and cities; how could she keep feeding us with lettuces and tubers and soy paste and that whole collection of fetid cheeses full of worms that were left for us in boxes on the welcome mat, he was going to make her pay, pay with her body so she would have a reason to whimper. Mom replied that if this was about paying, she was

the one who paid, she was the one who had funds in the bank
while he'd been unemployed for months. That money pained
Dad, that money made him kick the walls, made him bellow
his threats. One more potato and I'll mash it in your eyes, you
hear me?, one more carrot, and it's up your nose, he muttered
through his teeth so we couldn't hear him from the living room.
We heard him clearly through the walls and we could almost see
him burning Mom's pretty face with a boiling yam or suffocating
her with lentil puree. He always attacked her about the food and
Mom raised her voice in self-defense, not caring that her irate
shouts pierced our sides.

M om lowered her voice and finally confronted him. Where
did he want her to get that meat he insisted on eating, all
that infected meat that was going to make us sick and kill us if he
didn't kill us first. And when she saw him silent and diminished
she took the chance to tell him to figure out for himself where
to get the funereal hamburgers and the ribs that had turned him
into a raving lunatic. What kind of example are you setting for
the children? Aren't you such a man? Act like a man, then, she
told him furiously, and Dad's head sank further into his shoulders
and showed us a lamentable bald spot that we would have liked to
caress. But we didn't have time to get near Dad. He straightened
up without looking at her and left the kitchen. He retreated to
his room, to his computer, to his desperation, and he came out a
few hours later to announce that he had bought a gun. A pistol?
Mom started to cry while Dad proclaimed contemptuously that
his gun would arrive the next day, in a wooden box that was very
big and very heavy. A rifle? Mom trembled as she clutched the
pot she couldn't bring herself to wash. Dad sank into his silence,
again in his room, and Mom made space for herself in our bed
that night. No one got a wink of sleep because we couldn't fit on

the mattress, and because we were anxious to see the dawn arrive with its long box, with its long and shiny rifle that could hold more bullets than we could count. Dad crossed the cartridges over his chest and under his jacket, and he hoisted up that rifle he'd never seen before much less touched, a rifle he didn't know how to fire, and he went out and slammed the door behind him. Mom locked herself in the bathroom and vomited, imagining all the blood and all the meat she was going to have to cook for us, and eat with us, eat in front of us, with her eyes wide open over the plate. Dad's rifle pointed at her head.

Mom let him go without even a see you soon or a take care. She closed and bolted the door, and stood listening to his footsteps on the stairs. From the window we watched him appear on the street; he paused on the corner and turned around to wave, but he tripped over the ducks that had installed themselves behind him. There was a flurry of squawks and insults, and Dad kicked two or three with his boots while we secretly begged him to grab a duck by the neck and throw it to us as a consolation prize we could eat that night, even if we had to pluck it and stick it in the pot ourselves, without any help from Mom. But Dad didn't waste time on the ducks, no, Dad had equipped himself for larger game, and he was already moving off away from us. We saw him shrink in the distance and disappear among other men with long guns who were loaded down with munitions, men like him, without children, without women, without anything to lose. Mom!, we shrieked as soon as we realized that Dad was unprotected, Mom, Mom! Terrified, seeing the mask dangling from the doorknob, we ran to find her in her kitchen refuge to tell her Dad had gone out without his face cover. He could get sick, we said. Yes, children, he could die, Mom murmured with a grimace of disgust frozen on her face, as she stirred a pot of rice with water and a little sugar, no cinnamon sticks.

Mom told us not to worry, to stop looking out at the street, but when she saw us wandering around aimlessly she gave us permission to spend our days looking out for Dad's return. We kept watch from the heights of our open window, then our closed window, then open, then closed, closed, closed, because the air was starting to grow cooler. Mom saw us stationed there and then she was the one who wandered around us. She'd come up behind us, whisper into the napes of our necks that a watched pot never boils, and that Dad would come back one of these days, when we least expected it. That Dad wouldn't get sick and the poor wolves wouldn't eat him. Wolves? We hadn't even thought about wild wolves, but she had, she'd imagined the wolves skinning Dad, she'd wished for them to tear him apart, we could hear it in the murky depths of her voice. Mom was afraid we would see him coming from a distance, that among all the armed men in the street, one would turn out to be Dad. Because the outdoors must have turned him into one more animal. But the pot was boiling on the stove and Mom cooked the vegetables that arrived ever more sporadically, and the days passed, and the wind picked up and spilled leaves from the trees by the hundreds. Piles of leaves turning yellow before they rotted on the pavement with no one to sweep them. Dried leaves that the rain dragged off toward the gutters. And the snow began to cover the streets no one cleared, the rusted cars emptied of the gas that used to start them up. Across the snow, we'd say to ourselves, Dad would come walking with a deer on his shoulders, or at least one of those skunks that smelled so bad but had such tender flesh. So lovely, their fur.

* * *

Mom was untangling her shiny black hair with her thin fingers while she looked at us from the kitchen and begged us to sit down to eat her noodles with oil and the last, dried-out tomatoes. Losing her patience, she warned us that very soon, violent hail would start to fall, the windows would be smashed, what do you want, children, you want to let shards of glass rain down on you so your skin can get infected, now that there's no more medicine? Lose your eyes, is that what you want? No, we didn't want to lose anything, not our tongues or a hand and much less an eye, we'd already lost pounds, molars, hair. We had lost Dad, but not our hunger. We closed the blinds and the curtains suspecting that Dad had forgotten about us, that Dad had hunted and killed deer and bears and he'd eaten them on his own or in the company of other men armed to the teeth. We swallowed Mom's insipid noodles thinking that perhaps the one who'd been hunted down was him, because outside, any slipup could be deadly. That was the price of flesh—one's own. We didn't get sad thinking about it, nor were we happy. We didn't feel anything for Dad anymore. Just a calculation on our protruding ribs of how many days had passed. If we didn't go out it was because we remembered what we'd learned before school was shut down, what we'd been taught by the teacher—so robust, she'd been, with such thick hands. The food chain, she'd taught us. That teacher Mom had scorned for being fat had told us it was a law of nature to eat other animals, and that they, large or small, would eat us, before or after. She didn't tell us when the time would be right, but she insisted that someday our flesh would be feasted on by the worm species, and that eventually we'd become part of the bushes and the fruit trees that fed other animals. Someday we would be zebras or giraffes running through the parks. Mom liked that part of the lesson, she always applauded at that point, asked us to tell her the story again, and we would repeat it, changing some parts. The night when we were going to be camels, Mom smiled, her face a little fallen and hollow-eyed but still beautiful, and she said, someday, children, when we can go out, we'll go to the zoo and we'll find a caged monkey there, furiously shaking the bars, a monkey with green eyes just like your father's.

Mom didn't mention him again and maybe it was better, for the best, that Dad didn't come back. Vegetables were growing scarcer and there was no longer any way to get flour, yeast, milk, rice, and the fewer the mouths the more there was for each of us. Plus, Dad ate for a whole army. Mom opened the cupboards as if they were nocturnal windows emptied of stars. She closed the cupboards and soothed our hungry sleeplessness by telling us how giant and nearly extinct tortoises had begun to spawn again in the hot sand by the sea, fearless now with no egg hunters around, no tourists or overbearing bathers who were all the same thing: men. Men? Enormous, edible eggs stolen by hungry men? What did Mom mean? Weren't we men, too? Not you, replied Mom, you are only children. But we were men, small men, though not so small as we'd once been, and if we didn't die first we would turn into grown men whom Mom detested. Mom listened to the radio and repeated to us what she learned from it, that life on earth was composed of infinite plants and germs, of finite species, and very minimally by men, who had taken it upon themselves to end everything. That cannot be, she said. That's why the end of men is coming, my sweet boys, the revenge of the species is coming.

Mom, we said, staring at her skin so taut and smeared with oil, at the weave of her muscles over the bones. Her veins lit up. Mom, we repeated, infuriated, the men have already started to die, they're being devoured by wolf packs and birds of prey and worms; there are men rotting in the streets under clouds of flies. It's about time, Mom murmured with jumpy eyes, crushing a breadcrumb with a finger and depositing it on her tongue. Mom, we insisted, knowing it was useless, they're out in the streets looking for food and they collapse on the sidewalks, those men who aren't even men anymore. Mom pretended not to hear what we were saying, twirled her greying hair around a finger while we thought about all those cadavers stuck into freezers, all that meat in the now-empty meatpacking factories that were functioning as morgues. Meat that would be lost when the electricity went out. So much wasted meat. We said nothing, but our desperation must have shown through because Mom got up from the table, went to the door, and locked it with the only key in the house, and the key remained in the fist that Mom hid behind her back. She looked at us with feverish eyes, told us not to dare come near her, we were no match for her, even though she knew that skinny as she was, we could easily pick her up, we could force her arm, take away the key. We would open the door, go down the stairs, and disappear down the foggy neighborhood streets. Mom, we said, advancing slowly toward her, Mom, be good, give us the key, stand aside, let us out. We almost couldn't talk to her without salivating, we almost couldn't look at her in her torn nightgown, her arms bare, the stiff hairs of her underarms sticking out around the edges. It was better not to see her like that while she told us that we weren't her children anymore, but dirty, bloody men, carnivorous like Dad. But, she said haughtily, she wasn't going to allow us to go out that door. She opened her mouth and swallowed the key as if it were made of air, showed us her empty tongue. Her juicy tongue. She pressed her lips together, and then she smiled at us, baring her gums. And we smiled, too, astonished by what she had just done, admiring her quickness and cunning, adoring her determination and beauty, realizing that there was only one way we were leaving that house and it was by eating Mom.

164

Ariadne in Bloomingdale's

JULIA ALVAREZ

NEW YORK CITY, FALL 1971

You remember the little book of Greek myths
where we read about gods and goddesses,
their over-the-top, telenovela lives,
their cavorting and carrying on,
the rapture and rape of pubescent girls
in meadows, gathering flowers,
leaving a petal trail for their distraught mothers?
The mortal heroes were equally poorly behaved,
bullies marauding the beach, kicking down sandcastles.
I sighed with newly acquired condescension,
secretly thrilled by the naughty lives they were leading.
Goodbye & good riddance to the old stories!
They sunk to the murky bottom where a lot
of my useless education seemed to be going.
Now and again, one floated to the surface:
a beautiful housemate, a dead ringer for Helen;
a former flame who drank like a Dionysus;
briefly, I dated Adonis, a male model
with such eye-popping looks we both stared
at *his* reflection as we passed by a storefront window.
Turns out we don't get rid of that stuff—like a gas
it slips in under the padlocked door of the past
and what we thought academic can become
the story of our lives. The fall after graduation
I found myself living in Queens in my parents' house,

killing time before setting out for my Ithaca.
I got as far as Manhattan on my afternoons off,
riding the E or F train, murmuring names
as if reciting Homer's roll call of ships: *Parsons,*
Jackson Heights, Queensbridge, Roosevelt Island . . .
shedding my life at home, my Argus-eyed parents,
with each local or express stop. Sometimes the train
stalled in the dark tunnel and I saw myself
already changing shapes in my reflection,
becoming that nimble girl in the labyrinth
with a spool of thread and a road-map imagination.
Something important was about to happen,
worthy of my romantic education:
either a great love would sweep me away
(how I got waylaid by the fashion model)
or an impresario editor would discover
I was a female Orpheus in the making.
I had to get going, most of my favorite poets
had written their major works by their early twenties.
Keats would be dead of TB in a couple of years,
Shelley already married, Wordsworth done
with his *Lyrical Ballads*—I kept track of everyone's ages.
Back on the island my primas were getting married,
setting up households, expecting a first child.
Don't waste your brief looks on books, they counseled.
By the time we entered Manhattan, my head was spinning
as if I were being pursued by a gang of Furies.
Climbing the stairs, I blinked in the bright sunlight,
turned in confused circles, dizzy with options:
Where was my real life likely to be waiting?
Riven by indecision, I headed north
to the store with the promising name
where I could pretend another life for myself
at least for the afternoon, strolling the aisles,
mother-of-pearl, coral, ebony, amber,
a would-be Persephone on a shopping spree
in that underworld of artificial lighting,
returning home at dusk to Demeter Mami.
The pretty petite salesladies seemed aggrieved

at having to wait on the likes of me,
looking me over, their kohl-eyes calculating
where I had bought the outfit I was wearing:
bargains from Gertz or Mays, hand-me-downs
from a rich cousin or a well-heeled girlfriend.
Can I help you, Madam? they lisped. Madam?
I'd barely gotten the braces off my teeth!
I'd play my part, dismissing them with a breezy,
No, thank you, as if my chauffeur were waiting
in the line of town cars idling on a side street.
At a cosmetics counter an aging goddess
was having her face made over, free of charge.
Sometimes a model promoting a new perfume
offered to spray me, or proffered a doll-size sample,
but I resisted, finding the scent distracting.
First stop was the bargain basement, but even the sales
were overpriced: thirty bucks for a camisole!
How many books of poetry couldn't that buy?
On the other hand, which choice would attract guys?
In order to break the impasse, I ascended
to the upper carpeted floors where the drapes were drawn,
and the salesladies gave me that look again,
a look their great grandmothers might have cast
at an immigrant peddler. Designer outfits hung
each under a spotlight like paintings in a museum,
instead of crammed in racks like peasants in steerage.
I sailed on, intent on my destination,
a nook of a bookstore, tucked away
in the last available piece of real estate,
stocked with the usual suspects: bestsellers,
New Yorker anthologies with witty poems
whose allusions I never got; coffee-table books
with glossy shots of the wonders of the world—
Alps, pyramids, Parthenon—all transformed
into a kind of travel porn; one time
a copy of Dylan Thomas's poems.
I wandered the narrow aisles, checking out
what the rich were reading. Oh poverty of fine books!
Or maybe they weren't intended to be read—

only to serve as accents in a room?
All the time I was browsing, the thread of a life
that hadn't yet happened, that I didn't know
would happen or where I should go to find it
was tugging at me the way a memory might.
What if I never arrived in that glorious world
I only knew secondhand from the little book
stored in my parents' garage, and instead stayed trapped
in these blooming dales, hearing the Minotaur roar
of the midnight crew running their monstrous vacuums—
the life of any number of exiled tías,
cleaning the high rises, sewing in factorías,
unless I got out in time, racing past
camisoles, creams, sirens seductively calling,
mother-of-pearl, coral, ebony, amber,
and made my way out of the beautiful maze
to what would become this story of my life?

LANA BASTAŠIĆ is a Yugo-slav-born writer. Her first novel, *Catch the Rabbit,* won the European Union Prize in Literature in 2020 and was published in English in 2021. *Mliječni zubi* (Milk Teeth), a collection of short stories, was published in Serbo-Cro-atian in 2020.

CELIA HAWKESWORTH taught Serbian, Croatian, and Bosnian language and literature at the School of Slavonic and East European Studies, University of Lon-don, from 1971 to 2002. Since retiring she has been working as a freelance trans-lator. She began translating fiction in the 1960s, and to date has published transla-tions of some forty titles.

Bread

LANA BASTAŠIĆ
TRANSLATED FROM THE BOSNIAN BY
CELIA HAWKESWORTH

You're fourteen. You don't like these slacks, but someone once said you looked *awesome* in them and that's enough to make you put them on today, so in the mirror there's at least an idea, if not a whole person. When you were little you said *flacks* and everyone laughed, but there was tenderness in that laughter because it contained the idea that the mistake would stop when you were older. Now you're fourteen, standing in *awesome* slacks and looking at an ungainly body in the mirror. The mirror is small, its edges mean your legs below the knee and one shoulder are cut off. In the mirror is a mutilated body, and inside that body is you. The contradictions in your reflection are more painful than the overtight slacks. You bleed hot, thick blood out of too small a body. Between the stocky legs of a little furled girl you carry a sharp bush that no one has yet seen. Not even mum, not even a doctor. You're afraid of your bush because you're convinced other little girls don't have one. They're probably smooth down there, there must be something wrong with you. All the others are taller than you and almost all have breasts. Their fingers aren't little girls' fingers any more, they hold pencils as though they were cigarettes, they sway when they walk, they know how to pluck their eyebrows. You once tried to fix yours, but you overdid it and dad was furious. He asked whether you wanted to be a whore when you grew up. You shook your head. You stared at your plate, mum and your brother said nothing, the restaurant was full of little girls with perfect eyebrows. They're not going to be whores, you thought. They haven't got bushes down there or inside them. They're smooth. But eyebrows grow and now in the mirror yours are huge again. You try flattening them with your fingers and then you see your nails, cut to the quick, because you play the guitar and you're not allowed to have nails. Once you put polish on them and dad was furious. He said he knew a lot about the world and a girl who used nail polish at fourteen would be pregnant by sixteen. That's why your nails are colourless and cut off so that you're constantly aware of them. That pain is the pain of the edge, where the flesh stops and blood begins. You carry that pain in your fingers all the time, whatever you touch. You touched your lips, they're rough and peeling. Mum gave you lip balm and said you should carry it with you always as chewed lips aren't nice. That's because you chew them and press them together whenever anyone looks at you. And someone's always looking at you: teachers, girlfriends, boys, older boys, the woman next door, mum, dad. You can always be sure of other people's eyes on you wherever you are, that's why you'll always munch on your lips. It's easier than talking. Cooking, you have to learn: talk less or your lunch will burn, your gran once told you when you were making biscuits together. Gran had cracked lips as well, she didn't talk much either, but her breasts were enormous above the firm knot of her faded apron. You wouldn't have been able to carry them, you're sure they'd break your back. You're afraid of those breasts of gran's and of those few black hairs on her small, protruding chin. There's no time for chatter, lunch must be made, she says brightly, opening the oven. Her breasts hang almost to its shelves. When you were little, you thought the oven might swallow up gran and her big breasts. You think about that now as you look at your tight sweatshirt with a slogan you don't understand. Cool, the prettiest little girl in the class said when you came to school in that sweatshirt last week. No, she's not a little girl, but a young lady. She's already a young lady. You'd like to have her hair: long and straight, without a tiresome kink above her forehead. When you were at the photographer's, mum licked her fingers and yanked that kink so hard it gave you a headache. That was for a family photo, that pain in your skull. You feel it now every time you look at the photo. You have the feeling you can see mum's spit in your hair as well. You once washed your hair with something called *colour-shampoo* and then on your summer holiday you sought out the sun to catch the red sparks on your head. You wanted to have something to show that was yours and wasn't ordinary, boring. But that didn't last long because you were afraid dad would notice. You washed your hair with hot water every morning so as to kill the red colour before he saw it. The heat scalded the crown of your head, but you put up with it because even the weakest ray of sun would have been enough to ruin yet another family mealtime. Now you're here, in the mirror, ordinary again, hair brown as a dried chestnut again, with overlarge eyebrows and a kink in your hair and cracked lips. Your *awesome* slacks and your *cool* sweatshirt are unobtrusive enough to be taken out of this small room. You pass mum in the kitchen and dad on the couch and go outside. Because it's Saturday and you have to get bread. It's only a few minutes' walk down your street, but you know that your town is a beehive of eyes and that you will chew your lips and your tongue and your cheeks if someone looks at you today and doesn't see exactly the you who looked good enough in the frame of the mirror, good enough for dad not to have stopped you before you reached the door, good enough for the prettiest girl in the class to say you're cool. No matter if it's just an outing for a loaf of bread. You've done the shopping and now you're walking proudly with a warm bag in your hand, the pavements are deserted, the sun is so strong you're convinced it will reveal the last hints of red colour-shampoo in your hair. The street is empty and you feel you can be anything you want. You wonder whether that's the way real women feel, tall women, women with breasts, when they go to buy bread. And then you feel a heavy arm round your shoulders and another hand on your elbow. You don't know them, but they must come from round here, they stink of sweat and alcohol. Their closeness is like your cutoff nail, almost painful, the blood is right here, at the edge. At first you don't understand why they're so close to you, but then they start talking, panting into your ear and then you get it. You're all walking along your street which is suddenly emptier than it was, although a moment ago you were the only person in it, and now there are three of you. Sharp hairs scratch your face. They say you've got a nice bum, the one you'd seen earlier in the mirror, in the awesome flacks, no, in the slacks, the bum of a little fourteen-year-old girl who's conscious of her bush. But now you'd like to set fire to all the bushes in yourself and fold up like a box into one simple flatness. You want to be reduced to two dimensions just so that these words in your ears disappear and this chin against your cheek and this hand on your elbow and this stench that scours your nostrils. Your street is even emptier, the houses are like boxes, like you too, behind their windows there are no more eyes, the mothers are in their kitchens, the fathers are watching the news. You must do this on your own. He keeps on talking. Now he's telling you what he'd do to you, what he and his mate would do to you, and you don't want to cry, because then you'd be a small girl again who can't say *slacks* and then everything that's happening would be even harder. You have to put up with this, like that boiling water that kills the red in your hair, you have to hold out until you get to the door that's almost here, quite close. You have to stop: in your feet, your legs, your stomach, your elbows, your lungs, your hair; *you* have to stop completely. And you've succeeded, now you're just a reflection walking along the street, that body from the mirror, but without you in it. A body that's seen, touched, discussed, cursed, mocked, caught. A body that's walking in those slacks, in that sweatshirt, a body that's bearing his heavy hand on its shoulders. The body is reaching the door and unlocking it while those two guys go on their way with a few last remarks: about the lips of that body and the throat of that body and what all they would shove into that body. The body carries a bag with warm bread in it, the body hurts because today blood is gushing out of it, the body climbs the stairs and begins to shake in its two dimensions like a crumpled banknote in the wind. The body enters its father's house and now it's wild, bloody, sweaty, crying, and its father takes it in his arms and asks what happened. The body doesn't tell its father exactly what happened because all that happened were words which the body doesn't want to repeat, because the body is ashamed of itself in those words. The body feels that the body is to blame, it came out of the frame of the mirror and went into the street to buy bread wearing *awesome* slacks. It should have stayed inside, without legs or one shoulder. But the father holds the body, the father loves it and protects it. Protects it from the street, protects it from bushes. The father strokes its hair and says softly: Who's my girl? My little girl. And the body shrinks until it's small enough to fit into its father's hands and its father's question. The bushes wilt within the body and blood returns to the damaged tissue and its nails are once again as soft as a newborn's. The body subsides in its father's embrace while its mother slices the warm bread in the kitchen. Because today's Saturday and it's time for lunch.

RICKEY LAURENTIIS was raised in New Orleans, Louisiana, to love the dark. *Boy with Thorn*, their debut book, won the Cave Canem Poetry Prize, the Levis Reading Prize, and was a finalist for the Kate Tufts Discovery Award. Other honors include fellowships from the Lannan Literary Foundation, the National Endowment for the Arts, the Poetry Foundation, the Whiting Foundation, and the Center for African American Poetry and Poetics at the University of Pittsburgh.

The way the tides

RICKEY LAURENTIIS

Changed. Done
  Changed. Did. Did been.
Do. The woo
      They
Do opon the shores,
  The mercy that isn't taken against
Thy cliff
    Be
How, the ways
  In which, such privilege, and thusly
Y'all all
    Changed
In respect,
  Apparently, to gender
Entering me.
      Days
Some start with little or
  Less gender; other days overwhelm.
Why, yes, today
       Is
Very gendered! The air
  Bethicked right salt
Of it, and free
      And
Everywhere
  I look! Some days go

Restlessly, I remember,
                    And
I begin again the woes'
    Whoing me up, a sun
Across a fog,
                    Desire,
Dolores and Truth,
    The blue way
An ocean revises the shore,
                            Hinges,
Hinges that are the birds flying,
    My very skin, black, growing
Softer
        On
Each spill of a pill, breasts, lips,
    The conjugation of
My waist, my
                    Hips,
And so daybreak
    Breaks over me,
Apparent, a new woman,
                            Venus
Out of the grammared
    Pearl and waves
To you, waves,
                    Waves—
It's no longer then
    You see me. No,
You sea me.

Author, translator, and critic, CRISTINA RIVERA GARZA's recent publications include *Grieving: Dispatches from a Wounded Country*, which was named a finalist for the National Book Critics Circle Award in criticism; *The Restless Dead: Necrowriting and Disappropriation*; *La Castañeda Insane Asylum: Narratives of Pain from Modern Mexico*; and *Autobiografía del algodón*. She is Distinguished Professor and founder of the PhD Program in Creative Writing in Spanish at the University of Houston, Department of Hispanic Studies and a MacArthur Fellow of 2020.

FRANCISCA GONZÁLEZ-ARIAS has taught Spanish and courses on literature by Spanish and Latin American women writers for many years. Among her translations are works by Soledad Puértolas and Cristina Rivera Garza. She also translates from English to Spanish, most recently selected poems of Emily Dickinson. She lives in Cambridge, Massachusetts.

Dream Man

CRISTINA RIVERA GARZA
TRANSLATED FROM THE SPANISH BY
FRANCISCA GONZÁLEZ-ARIAS

Strange things always happened to him with her, but what surprised him most was the way in which he would stop loving her for long periods, sometimes for whole years. During that time his lack of love would become an almost natural discipline: he'd walk unhurried, play with his son in the morning, read the newspapers, work, or chat with friends in trendy restaurants, both complain about, and enjoy, life. At those times, Fuensanta, his wife, would smile more and sleep better. Whenever she came upon him unawares on the balcony, leaning on the iron railing with his gaze lost in the treetops, she didn't ask him, "What are you thinking about, Álvaro?" Instead, she'd run her hand over his shoulder and move away, sure of herself, without suspecting anything. But then, without any obvious reason, it would happen once more: he loved her again. At times the emotion was provoked by the smell that wafted from the bakery on certain July afternoons. Sometimes everything began to happen again because, by chance, someone said words that he had heard only on her lips. *Solanum tuberosum*. At other times, he'd receive messages, brief notes written on onion skin paper or monosyllabic telegrams that fluttered onto his desk weightlessly like the swaying of a dry leaf. They were the signs of her proximity.

At those moments he studied his own life, and with unpremeditated urgency he'd appeal to grandmothers and aunts in search of information. He wasn't completely sure of what he was looking for, but he couldn't rest until he found it. And so, between mugs of hot chocolate and sweet rolls, or in the middle of big family meals that took place over long wooden tables, he'd listen once again to stories of his childhood with feigned inattentiveness. He had been a happy child. Born in the month of April in the bosom of a stable family, he had never wanted for anything. He had had more than enough light, nourishment, pampering, bedtime stories, and the affectionate pats with which anyone awakened by a nightmare is lulled back to sleep. His needs had not been excessive and for that reason he developed an even and placid temperament, given to good company and easy laughter. Since he was the youngest of three children and the only boy, he soon became his mother's and father's favorite, although for different reasons. His early years transpired without mishap among loving relatives, vacations at the seaside, and books. Right between dessert and coffee, but still under the influence of those stories, he verified once more what he already knew: there was no pathology in his life that could have led him to her. No trauma or complex predisposed him to seek her presence.

But that was not what he felt the first time he loved her. It happened in the winter, during one of the most pleasant periods of his life. He had finished his university degree in engineering and had married a woman with gentle manners and a true gaze. Still childless, the newlyweds spent time enjoying their bodies in different landscapes. They liked to travel. Sometimes they would opt for grand voyages across continents while other times they'd take short weekend getaways to neighboring cities. They'd go to Cholula, Cuernavaca, or Tepoztlán, guided by strong intuitions rather than specific plans. On those occasions they drove carefully, listened to music by dead composers, and admired the mountainsides monosyllabically. One of those trips took them to Toluca, a high-altitude city whose greatest charm was the cold. There they stayed in a small, graceless hotel and a little before nightfall, instead of having a bite to eat and going to bed, they decided to put on their coats and take a walk under the arcades of the City Hall. The cold made them quicken their pace and lock arms energetically.

"My bones ache," said Fuensanta, rubbing her hands, "I'd rather go back."

"I'll go with you," Álvaro hastened to reply.

"But this is what you came for, Álvaro, to walk in the cold." Fuensanta reminded him of his wish and pushed him toward the sidewalk, urging him on.

Still undecided whether to let her return to the unfamiliar hotel or continue his walk in the wind, he saw her recede little by little until she disappeared around a corner. The cold, which had the virtue of putting him in a good mood, made him react with unaccustomed energy. He turned, lengthened his stride and more rapidly than usual he crossed the downtown area without paying too much attention to the few nocturnal passersby or the buildings characteristic of a drab, and perhaps too new city. Spurred on by the gusts of wind that were coming from the snow-covered Nevado de Toluca volcano, Álvaro left the downtown area and penetrated the steep and asymmetrical streets that came and went without warning. Soon he didn't have the slightest idea where he was, but instead of worrying him, the disorientation and the cold sharpened his senses: he was as awake as he had ever been, and for that reason content. It was while in that state of physical and mental alertness that Álvaro saw her for the first time.

It was already past ten when he began to feel tired. As fatigue overcame more and more of his body, he paid greater attention to his surroundings. There were squat shabby houses with big iron gates, fried food stands where people milled around the fire, pharmacies, neon signs, stairs. Trying to get his bearings, he came closer to a lamppost but the light disappeared as soon as he reached it. At that moment he became aware of the danger. He was in an unknown neighborhood in a strange city late at night. In addition, it was cold; a sharp, overwhelming, pitiless cold. He turned in every direction trying to find a taxi but the street was deserted. Desperate, he approached a couple of nocturnal pedestrians to ask them the fastest way to reach the city center, but neither of the two looked him in the eyes, and they passed by his side without saying a word. Still excited by the cold, but beginning to feel afraid, Álvaro went up a steep slope until, breathless, he was forced to stop and vomit because of the effort. He was bending down in front of a small window when he heard moans: it was the faint sound of two people who had just made love. Then, forgetting his situation, he peeked in between the slats of the blinds and observed them. A half-dressed man and woman were still intertwined. The weak light of the lamp and the purplish brocade of the sofa lent the scene the patina of an almost unbearably remote past. There were numerous golden statuettes on rectangular tables as well as oil paintings with thick wooden frames hanging on the white walls.

While the man hurriedly zipped up his pants and knotted his tie in front of an oval mirror, the woman lay immobile on the sofa. Perhaps she was waiting for something: a word or a caress. But nothing came. From under a dress of sky-blue silk emerged a long white leg ending in a high-heeled shoe of the same pastel tone. Then, as if she had sensed his presence, the woman let her head fall back over one of the edges of the sofa, and stared directly at the minuscule orifice of the window. Irregular bangs flowed over her temples, crowning a pair of big translucent eyes. Álvaro was sure he had been seen and ran away. Once again with labored breath he reached what seemed to be an expressway, and there he stopped the first taxi he saw.

"I'm going downtown," he said, "to the Guardiola Hotel."

The taxi driver gazed at him in the rearview mirror with a look of complicity but didn't ask any questions. Then he lit a cigarette and turned up the radio. Conchita Velázquez's most famous song filled Álvaro with melancholy. The lyrics reminded him of the scene he had just witnessed, and he imagined that the couple in the old house had made love *as if tonight were the last night*. An air of uselessness, an aura of lost time, an echo of urgency hovered over them. When he finally arrived at the hotel, Álvaro paid and, upon opening the door, was surprised by the cold once again.

"But it's so cold," he said, more to himself than to the taxi driver.

"Well, what do you expect, it's midnight at the end of November," answered the man without taking the cigarette out of his mouth.

At that moment he thought of the absurd garb of the woman on the sofa: a sky-blue silk dress on a winter's night, a dress with narrow straps in a place like Toluca, the city with the highest elevation in the entire country. Then he turned up his coat collar and crossed the street.

Fuensanta was asleep, and she did not wake when he slowly settled himself under the covers. He tried to get closer to glean some heat from her but restrained himself since his hands and feet were like chunks of ice and he didn't want to disturb her.

Immobile, with his eyes open in the darkness, Álvaro waited a long time for a warmth that did not come. Then he heard the staccato of high heels on the floor tiles in the hallway, and without knowing why, he hugged Fuensanta as if she were his salvation.

"It's nothing," he whispered in his wife's ear when she opened her eyes.

"Did you finish what you had to do?" she asked with a sleepy smile on her lips before shutting her eyes again.

Despite the innocence of the question, Fuensanta's words put him on the defensive. What was it that he "had to do"? Trying to find the answer, he fell asleep.

The morning light forced him to change his position on the bed several times, until fed up with the sun's relentless pursuit he decided to get up when there was no longer any shade under which to find refuge. Grudgingly, he opened his eyes, and the empty room overwhelmed him. Fuensanta was no longer under the blankets or any other place. He was going to call her when he saw the note on top of the bureau. *I'm going for a walk and then I'll have lunch in the hotel dining room. Meet me there a little before twelve. Kisses, Fuensanta.* The little hands on the clock indicated that it was still possible for him to get there on time. He had a quick bath and put on some faded jeans and a plaid shirt. The image he saw in the mirror was that of a normal man.

All around the room were big clean windows through which the clear and sharp light of the highlands penetrated. Álvaro searched for Fuensanta's face among the diners, and when he saw her half-watermelon smile he realized that she wasn't alone. Fuensanta was sharing a light lunch with another woman.

"Look, Álvaro, this is Irena," said Fuensanta as soon as she saw him.

There was an excitement in her voice like that of someone who has found a treasure or the correct name of a street in a city without street signs. The stranger raised her face and Álvaro was unable to pronounce a single word. Mute, immobile, afraid of being exposed, he could barely manage to look at her. She no longer wore the absurd silk dress but a pair of brown corduroy overalls over a white T-shirt that made her seem much younger. Chestnut colored bangs covered her forehead and framed the same big, sad eyes that he had seen the night before. Her ponytail and a simple amethyst necklace gave her the look of an old child. When Álvaro finally shook her hand, the noon light sparkled on feminine skin.

"Pleased to meet you," said Irena.

Her voice was exactly as he had imagined it: soft but deep, as if it emerged from moist zones below the stomach. In his confusion, Álvaro forgot that he was hungry.

"Álvaro, Irena knows this region very well," announced Fuensanta euphorically. "She's gathering wild plants from the foothills of the volcano, isn't that so, Irena? And she wouldn't mind if we accompany her today."

"Unless, of course, you'd rather just stay in the city and peep around the area."

Irena's words seemed transparent, but Álvaro knew immediately that they weren't. He had no doubt that she had seen him. *Peep.* He had been found out. But she wouldn't tell on him. That seemed to be the deal. Álvaro agreed to go up the mountain almost immediately: he had no other choice.

"It's getting a little late, but we still have a few hours of broad daylight left."

Irena guided them through narrow streets until they reached a cherry-colored pick-up truck. When the door was opened a cloud of dust made him cough. There were rusted tools on the floor, maps, compasses on the worn seats, and dirty napkins. Álvaro settled himself into the back as best he could, and Fuensanta became copilot.

"And these bags?" asked Álvaro, pointing to a pair of knapsacks full of cans and other tinned foods.

"It's my sustenance for this month," Irena explained, without letting up driving at what seemed excessive speed. "I have a cabin near Raíces. I spend almost all my time there, especially during the winter harvesting season. I don't come down to the city very often," she muttered between her teeth, looking at him in the rearview mirror.

"How interesting," said Álvaro, listening to her as one does to a liar.

The landscape distracted him. Light fell tenuous and sharp on the cornfields. In the distance the horizon was almost blue, and like the high sky, unreachable. Farther away, the volcano awaited them, fearless, secure, eternal. There was something threatening in the snow that covered it.

"It must be terribly cold at night," said Fuensanta. "You'd like to live around here, Álvaro, isn't that so?"

Before he answered, Fuensanta added: "Álvaro loves the cold, Irena. I don't know why."

Irena looked at him again in the rearview mirror; an unusual shimmer emerged from a crack in her pupils.

"It must be because no one can stay still in the cold," said the woman.

Álvaro lowered his eyes and considered running away.

Irena turned off the highway onto a dirt road. She drove for another stretch, avoiding the pine tree trunks until she stopped the vehicle in a totally green, solitary spot. Once there, Irena began to walk. Fuensanta and Álvaro followed close behind. The landscape captivated them. The pine trees that covered the mountainsides seemed to transport them someplace else, an enchanted forest where children get lost, the primeval, mythical forest. The pine trees blocked the sun's rays and soon the visitors were cold. Without paying attention to them, Irena stopped to examine closely a small flower with delicate lilac-colored petals.

"*Solanum tuberosum,*" she said, raising her face toward them as if she were repeating a magical lesson.

Fuensanta and Álvaro exchanged uncomfortable looks.

"Irena, we're freezing," explained Fuensanta with just a hint of impatience. In response, Irena stood up and walked hurriedly.

"There's only one way to get over that, Fuensanta"—she turned around to look at her— "Let's run."

The smile on Álvaro's face was a combination of fright and desire. He was beside himself, running downhill without thinking of his wife, without thinking of anything. His body had taken over and guided him up and down, as if a prize awaited him on the other side of the hill, and on the other side of his respiration. Breathing hard once again and with a fresh urge to vomit because of the altitude, Álvaro was almost dragging himself by the time he arrived at Irena's cabin. She was seated on a rock waiting for him, near a lamb which she treated with unusual familiarity. When he reached her, they smiled at each other, and were going to say something when they heard a scream.

"Álvaro!" Fuensanta's voice indicated that something serious had happened.

Without hesitation Irena went toward her and came back with Fuensanta leaning on her shoulder. She had sprained her ankle.

"Álvaro," Fuensanta mumbled when she came near him.

Her husband observed her as if through a thick fog and didn't move. It wasn't until the third or fourth time he heard his name that he stretched out his arms and carried her.

"Everything's all right," Álvaro stammered.

Irena opened the door of her cabin and invited them in. The fire in the fireplace made them quiet: its gentle heat and the orange light of the flames seemed eternal. While Irena bandaged Fuensanta's ankle with expert hands, Álvaro glided noiselessly through the space. He touched the stone and wood walls; caressed the book covers, the upholstery, and the curtains. Like a modern-day Saint Thomas, he touched everything in his path, trying to convince himself that it existed, that it was real. In some infinitesimal spot in his brain, deep within his dreams, there had existed a place like this. But he had never seen it before. He had never been inside it.

"What exactly do you do?" Álvaro asked with genuine curiosity, as he glanced at books on meteorology, issues of the journal of the Botanical Society of Mexico, theses on genetic improvement, and pencil sketches of very small plants.

"Irena does research for an agronomic institute, isn't that so?" interrupted Fuensanta.

The woman kept quiet until she finished adjusting the bandage around Fuensanta's ankle. Then, with visible signs of satisfaction on her face, she got up.

"Let's have a drink," she said, picking up a bottle of cognac and three glasses without waiting for a reply.

Between sips she explained that she was in charge of a census of wild species that grew on the slopes of the volcano for an agricultural research institute in Arizona. She was interested above all in potatoes. *Solanum tuberosum*. She worked for a team that was trying to find a non-chemical solution to the problem caused by the late-blooming *tizón*, a fungus which, among other things, had destroyed entire harvests in nineteenth-century Ireland, causing the famine that led to massive emigration to the United States. Irena illustrated her narration with leaves afflicted by the disease, bringing them closer for Álvaro and Fuensanta to view, as if they were myopic or genuinely interested in her scientific research. Little by little as her interlocutors' questions decreased,

Irena changed the topic. They spoke for a bit about the climate, and some more about Mexico City, and finally, they were quiet. The lamb's bleating made them jump up from their seats.

"We're far away from civilization," murmured Fuensanta, undoubtedly animated by the cognac.

"Yes," mumbled Irena. "Absolutely."

Álvaro didn't open his mouth except to ask for more alcohol. While the amber-colored liquid was poured into his glass, the image of Irena wrapped in a dress of sky-blue silk seemed even more absurd than it had the night before. Surely he had made a mistake. He must have seen something else. There was no connection between the woman in overalls who studied plants and the woman reclining on an antique sofa after having made love with a man who was undoubtedly cruel. His rapidly increasing curiosity kept him alert. Fuensanta, on the contrary, soon fell into a tipsy doze.

"You can stay here tonight," Irena said when she noticed Fuensanta's languor. "Tomorrow I'll take you back to civilization," she joked.

The wrinkles around her mouth aroused him. Her way of keeping still with her gaze fixed on the fire drove him crazy. With one thing and another, Álvaro realized that he wanted to get to know her. What is there beyond civilization? he asked himself in silence. Love, he answered immediately. Outside, all around him the primeval forest acquired the darkness of mystery. Or of terror, he added to himself.

It seemed that they wouldn't be able to return the next day either. A light snowfall and a problem with Irena's truck prevented them from going back down the mountain to the Guardiola Hotel, back to their car and to their normal life in Mexico City. Civilization. Irena prepared a lentil stew on a wood-burning stove, in between descriptions of conifers and helobial plants, and behaved like a perfect hostess. Everything in her behavior indicated that she was enjoying the extended company of the tourists. Far from feeling at ease, Fuensanta and Álvaro soon found themselves exchanging looks of deep anxiety.

"We have to get back today whichever way possible," Fuensanta said without worrying about good manners, tired of beating about the bush and broaching the subject in roundabout ways.

"Work, you know," Álvaro explained, trying to smooth over any unnecessary gruffness.

"I understand," their hostess answered with a smile on her lips but without doing anything else.

After eating, however, she went out to the pick-up carrying a toolbox. Álvaro volunteered to help, but she declined his offer.

"Fuensanta may need you," she said. "I won't be long."

In her absence, both Álvaro and Fuensanta automatically undertook an inspection of the place. Their curiosity made them break with pre-established social codes. The cabin, which had been a welcoming hut the night before, was now a hermetic cave, full of signs of decay and malignant air. However, nothing they found seemed important or stood out. The biology and botany books were arranged one after the other in perfect order; the *mazahua* rugs matched the onyx statuettes and other crafts from the surrounding areas. There were work boots next to the bed, thick woolen sweaters, and a pair of binoculars. Everything was in harmony with Irena's personality: her books, her silences, her projects. The cabin was completely hers. It fit her like a glove.

"Look," Fuensanta called to him, showing Álvaro a bundle of letters with stamps from Denmark. "They don't seem to be from Arizona."

Álvaro wasn't listening because in between the pages of a book on zoology he had just found the photograph of a man. He

194

was dressed in a sky-blue suit, and from underneath a thinly trimmed moustache emerged a pair of thick, sensual, almost brutal lips. The felt hat which covered his head seemed to belong to another time.

"It's him," he exclaimed. "So everything is true."

"What's true?" Fuensanta asked from the other side of the house. Álvaro hesitated for a moment, but finally decided to lie.

"That we're shut up in a cabin in the middle of an enchanted forest," he said in a jocular tone, putting the photo in one of his coat pockets.

Fuensanta didn't smile. Outside, a light layer of snow left white islands on the landscape and on memory. They observed the light of the mountains without saying anything; then they saw the sun beginning to set. A dizzying anguish forced them to keep quiet.

"And if we never get out of here?" Fuensanta asked with a mixture of regret and anger. "We should never have accepted this absurd invitation."

The choice of the term caught his attention. *Absurd.* He too had used it the night before. Despite the fact that nothing sinister could be detected and everything seemed in order, the word sprung up naturally. Irena was absurd. Her cabin in the middle of the enchanted forest was absurd. And there they were, hugging in front of the fireplace, sleepy with uneasiness, also absurd. The lamb's insistent bleating was absurd. And absurd too was the cold that had brought them to a city without charm, and to a sleeping mountain watched over by a dead volcano.

Irena returned a little after nightfall. She came hurriedly, in the company of a thin little man dressed in a red poncho.

"If it weren't for Ezequiel you'd have to stay here," she announced.

Hearing her mention him, the man lowered his eyes to hide his satisfaction. Then, without transition, Irena guided them back to the truck. Like the day before, Álvaro got in the back, while Fuensanta was in the copilot's seat from where she nervously observed the speedometer. As they went down the mountain the tall pines gave way to dry willows and later to the stoplights of the darkened city. Both of them breathed with relief when they reached the streets of the downtown area.

"Thank you for everything," Fuensanta said in a cutting tone as soon as she opened the door of the vehicle.

Irena smiled a crooked smile.

"The pleasure was mine," she said as if she were in reality saying something else, looking at the windshield.

Suddenly, as he placed his foot on the ground, Álvaro grasped with horror that Fuensanta didn't intend to give Irena their address or phone number in Mexico City. Everything seemed to indicate that she meant for the absurdities to end there, under a dark sky at the door of the Guardiola Hotel. At the last minute, just before following his wife, Álvaro turned and took out his wallet from his back pocket and with unpremeditated daring, extracted one of his cards.

"Look me up when you go to Mexico City," he said, in a natural tone that was obviously a sham.

Irena, however, took the card with an outstretched arm and an open hand, as if she had been waiting for it forever. Once again taken by surprise, Álvaro thought that Irena was in reality in a place outside civilization. And for that reason he loved her. One, two, five minutes. Then the cold forced them to say good-bye in monosyllables.

It took a month for Fuensanta's ankle to heal. As they resumed with difficulty the normal rhythm of their lives, both Álvaro and Fuensanta chose to omit the word Toluca from their conversations. Neither of the two pronounced Irena's name. Despite being absolute, the omission was not the result of any agreement, but rather of a fleeting sense of dread that made them close their eyes before actually falling asleep. At those moments, the two entered the enchanted forest through different paths. Fuensanta advanced above the landscape with slow cloudlike steps, while Álvaro ran among the trees at top speed.

In all his visions, Irena held his hand, gliding alongside him with the rhythm of a shadow, like something superimposed. Then, when Álvaro and Fuensanta woke up in the same bed, the two exited the forest in the same way.

Álvaro thought of Irena for a few days, an entire week perhaps. The image of the woman slipped in through the cracks in his schedule, with the onslaught of the cold, or the nostalgia for a green place. Sometimes, especially when he observed the tops of the trees from the terrace of his apartment on the thirteenth floor, he imagined that he loved her. The emotion that immobilized him then was huge. He trembled, experiencing a feeling of hunger in his mouth and stomach, followed immediately by an immense urge to vomit. Little by little, between family meals and television programs, he lost sight of her inside him. Then he forgot her, like one forgets those things that never happened.

Later, when Fuensanta and Álvaro didn't say the word Toluca, it wasn't due to precaution but rather to having given it up. The two of them had managed to find the exit from the primeval forest. But they were mistaken.

Álvaro caught sight of Irena a second time under the jacarandas of April. He had gotten together with Sonia, his older sister, in an open-air cafe where they had arranged to meet to catch up and talk about unimportant things as was their custom. Before ordering the requisite cappuccinos and deciding between the raspberry tart and the cheesecake, the two hastily opened a cigarette pack.

"If Fuensanta saw me doing this she'd kill me on the spot," said Álvaro with a cigarette lighter in his left hand.

Sonia shrugged her shoulders and urged him to continue with the bad habit they had begun a long time ago, at the start of adolescence's winding road.

"But she can't see us, Álvaro," commented his sister, while she exhaled smoke in the direction of his face with secret pleasure.

Whether it was to avoid the irritation from the smoke or to enjoy alone the taste of tobacco on his lips, Álvaro closed his eyes. One, two, five seconds. When he opened them he didn't see Sonia, but Irena. She was crossing the threshold of the doorway with her sky-blue silk dress, a pearl necklace, and the exhausted attitude of a cow on its way to the slaughterhouse.

"Did you see a ghost? You turned so pale."

When Sonia turned around in her seat to identify the cause of her brother's confusion it was too late. Irena was fleeing in a white limousine whose tinted glass prevented Álvaro from seeing inside. After the incident, brother and sister didn't have coffee or eat anything. Chain-smoking, Sonia tried to make sense of a story that Álvaro narrated in half-finished sentences, halting stammers, and ecstatic smiles.

"It's a woman, Sonia," he said to her. "A woman I met in a forest."

Sonia, who had been privy to her brother's romantic ups-and-downs for years, just kept quiet. There was something in the story that attracted and bothered her at the same time. It wasn't Irena's double life, or Fuensanta's ignorance, or the infantile tone with which Álvaro described his metaphysical affair.

"I didn't know you liked the cold so much, Álvaro." Finally she had hit upon the answer.

The story bothered her because it was based on information she was unfamiliar with. The person whom she thought she knew by heart was now slipping away from her because of a very small but essential reason: the cold. One always missed something.

"It's not such a big deal, Sonia," replied Álvaro without conviction.

The cold. He liked it, it's true, but he didn't know since when. It had been a sudden thing, he was sure; one of those convictions that are born, grow, reproduce at breakneck speed, and never die. Perhaps everything had begun that wintry morning in which the immobile city had covered itself with white clouds, trying to find a bit of warmth, and he, on the other hand, had taken to the street at a rapid pace, conquering the whole of it. Irena was right: during the cold, everything was permitted but movement was required. That was its charm, its particular fascination.

The chat with Sonia ended on a note of distrust as well as resignation. Despite the fact that all the words they exchanged had been gentle and reasonable, the two avoided looking each other in the eye when they walked together toward the garage.

"Keep me in the loop." Sonia laconically said good-bye.

The following day Álvaro found a bouquet of flowers and a manila envelope on his desk. The joy that invaded him was comparable only to his fear. What was Irena looking for? What could he give her? The image of a mad Irena, tied to his ankles like a steel ball, made him hesitate when he breathed in the aroma of the tuberoses that she had sent him. His office mates' curious gazes pierced the glass like thousand-year-old swords and that made him stop, open the envelope as if it had to do with a family matter, and read with a blend of patience and astonishment: *Meet me at the Café Siracusa at 4:15, Irena*. What bothered him most was the fact that she didn't seem to have the slightest doubt that he would keep the appointment.

The Café Siracusa was an old-fashioned place frequented mostly by mid-level office workers and women with big plastic bags. Álvaro went once in a while because it was only a few blocks from his place of work, and above all because no one knew him there. Whenever he wanted to escape or hide, he'd go to the Siracusa as if it were a secret paradise or a refuge frozen on the shores of time. The big prints of Greek theater, the temples of Apollo, and the Euryalus Fortress which covered the walls lent that effect. As always upon arriving he went to the bar, ordered a whiskey on the rocks, opened the newspaper and waited. This time he knew something was going to happen.

Irena arrived half an hour late with damp hair.

"I'm sorry, Álvaro." With her khaki slacks and blue shirt she almost seemed a normal woman. "But it's still difficult for me to gauge distances in this city."

It seemed like a logical excuse to Álvaro. "Let's go over there, is that OK?"

They moved to a table surrounded by some red overstuffed chairs. Irena ordered a sandwich and a bottle of mineral water. When the waitress left, the two realized that they had absolutely nothing to talk about.

"Why are you spying on me, Irena?"

The question was said by another person inside him, some impolite and tactless person, without the slightest sense of mystery and the complexities of seduction; someone who was afraid.

"You're the spy, Álvaro," Irena responded naturally, as if the topic of espionage were common between two people who were getting together for the first time without knowing each other yet. "Give me back Hercules's photograph," she added in a low voice, as if mentioning the topic were more painful for her than for him.

Álvaro opened the manila envelope and extracted the picture. "It was a stupid reaction," he said. "I didn't mean to keep it."

Álvaro had never felt as he did at that moment in the Siracusa, seated next to Irena for the first time: he was naked and he was unable to lie.

"I know," she said, caressing the back of his hand and making him look at her.

Then, like the strangers they were, they talked about the weather, not mentioning the man in the photograph or Fuensanta. Nor did Álvaro dare ask Irena what brought her to Mexico City, and she didn't volunteer any explanation. Without much to talk about, they ended up telling innocuous jokes. Both were in a good mood. When Irena finished her sandwich, and Álvaro his third whiskey, the two left the Siracusa without anything in particular in mind. Together, holding hands, bumping into people in a hurry, they seemed like children walking aimlessly, or two idle adolescents. It was almost dark when they came upon a park with dry plants and wilted chrysanthemums. They sat on the grass and continued their meaningless conversation. The weather. Both of them loved the cold. Then, without planning to, they stood up together, and kept walking until they found the Sorrento Hotel with its doors wide open. At 10:35 p.m. they made love for the first time.

They spent the next two days together. They'd have breakfast in the Siracusa and then walk without any fixed destination until hunger pangs brought them back to the Café. Then they'd play Chinese checkers on plastic boards, buy sunflower seeds, and strike up conversations with homeless people, and at night they'd make love with extraordinary calm. They acted as if they had all the time in the world or as if time had stopped forever at an island port. Álvaro phoned Fuensanta and, after failing to come up with a plausible lie, he simply asked her not to wait for him; that he would explain later. Neither Irena nor Álvaro acted like furtive lovers: they didn't hide or search for dark places to kiss with passionate hurry, and they didn't change their names. On the contrary, the two walked the city streets as if they were invisible. If someone had stopped to greet Álvaro, he would have said with the utmost naturalness:

"Surely you must be confusing me with somebody else. I'm not Álvaro Diéguez," and the interlocutor would have believed him.

If someone had grabbed Irena by the elbow, she would have excused the other person's error.

"You're mistaken, sir. My name is not Irena Corvián."

And both of them, in the strictest sense, would have been telling the truth.

When the moment to say good-bye came, they shook hands with no rush or dramatic gestures.

"Thank you for everything," said Irena.

"The pleasure was all mine," replied Álvaro.

Then he accompanied her to the parking garage where the cherry-colored pick-up was waiting for her. When he saw her leave, he realized that he knew almost nothing about her, and with relief, he was aware that he hadn't offered any unnecessary information either. Then, he walked back to his office, eyes cast down and a half-hidden smile on his lips. The aroma of the tube-roses confirmed to him that nothing had been a dream, but the note in the manila envelope made him wonder once again: *Don't kid yourself, Álvaro. I don't exist. Irena.*

Both Fuensanta and Álvaro had forgotten his inexplicable disappearance for two whole days when, by chance, he remembered the event. It was at one of those gatherings of good friends where familiarity and red wine lead inexorably to the discussion of controversial topics: gender inequality.

"And what would you do if you were men?" the men asked the women in a provocative tone, trying to put them between a rock and a hard place.

One of them, the wife of Álvaro's best friend, said frankly:

"I would be more attentive to the emotional needs of my wife." The subtext made more than one of them blush, and put others in a bad mood.

Immediately there were giggles.

"Well, if I were a woman," said the husband in question, "I would put on sexy nightgowns and make passionate love every night."

"Well if I were a man," insisted the same woman, "I would make a superhuman effort to learn how to listen."

As the volume of the matrimonial dialogue increased, the hosts moved around the table offering cigarettes and wine.

"And if you were a woman, Álvaro?" asked Fuensanta, more to silence the couple who were on the verge of an argument, than to find out what her husband thought.

Álvaro let out a nervous laugh, reached for his wineglass, and to the surprise and disapproval of his wife, accepted a cigarette. Then he kept quiet.

"So?" asked Sergio, the host, expecting a reply.

"I would wear sky blue, and forgetting would be easy for me." The silence around the table was as profound as his own astonishment.

Álvaro had just remembered Irena.

"And what in God's name does that mean?" asked the interrogated husband, trying to provoke something similar to his own conjugal quarrel.

"I don't know." Álvaro refused to say anything more.

He smiled at him, raised the cigarette to his lips and, a second later, exhaled the smoke with singular satisfaction. He had decided to go to the Nevado de Toluca one more time. Suddenly, he felt like running in the cold and telling stupid jokes.

"Well, if I were a man, I would be exactly as I am," Fuensanta informed the gathering, considering the matter closed.

Little by little, people left. The angry couple went away with remorseful expressions, and in the end only the hosts, as well as Álvaro and Fuensanta, remained, sitting in chairs on opposite sides of the living room.

"They seem to have problems," said Nélida, the hostess, resuming the thread of the conversation. "But who doesn't?"

"Discreet individuals," replied Álvaro with an ironic note in his voice, while he observed Fuensanta from the corner of his eye.

"Or otherworldly beings," added Sergio.

It was in this way that they eventually came to the subject of sirens. They spoke of Ulysses and the Mediterranean, and ears filled with wax; they made comments about firm-breasted mermaids that appeared on lottery tickets, discussed the one described by Hans Christian Andersen; and then, by chance, they ended up in the Toluca Valley.

"But there isn't enough water there," commented Álvaro, with genuine interest.

"There used to be," said Nélida, an anthropologist whom they knew had been researching the history of the Chanclana, a famous mermaid made of *tule*, or bulrushes, who, according to oral tradition, had the ability to destroy men.

Relishing the others' attention, the anthropologist described the ancient lakes of the region as "generous" and "inexplicably beautiful." Then she explained that although it dated from time immemorial, the legend of the mermaid had recently come into vogue among the fishermen when, due to the construction of a dam, the lakes had disappeared.

"A veiled criticism of modernity, no doubt," she determined.

It was in this way that they exited the territory of other-worldly beings and arrived at the more pressing, though more abstract, topic of postmodernism. Álvaro by then was on his third cigarette of the night without paying the least attention to his surroundings. A slight, blissful tipsiness repeated the name of Irena in his right ear.

Sirena.

Álvaro didn't return to Toluca until several months later. First, he had been incapable of finding a sufficiently logical pretext to explain his trip to a frigid valley without mentioning the name of the other woman. Then, he waited in vain for Fuensanta to go away for a weekend to Tepoztlán with her girlfriends from college. Finally, as the days and weeks passed, he forgot about it. He forgot that he had wanted to go up the mountain, high above the air, until he reached the season's snow. His tasks distracted him; his daily rituals fascinated him once more. When the possibility of going opened up in front of his distracted eyes, he couldn't believe it. It was the second weekend in November when Fuensanta announced with a smile that her parents had given her a ticket to go to Cancún.

"I suppose the heat will do you good," he said.

It was at that moment that Álvaro became aware of his chance: he would go in the direction of the opposite climate that his wife was traveling to.

Álvaro left Mexico City on a Friday at three in the afternoon. He was taking an extra pair of boots, his leather gloves, and a black coat inside the trunk of the car. He had even taken the precaution of buying a first aid kit. The music of Leonard Cohen accompanied him as he crossed the Desert of the Lions, and then, La Marquesa, *I'm your man.* The high green band of the pine trees, the blue of the sky, the lightness of the air. Everything that reminded him of a being inside himself that responded to the name of Irena. This was her context: an agglomeration of houses and people at the highest altitude in the country; a junction of Spanish broom where moisture had turned to stone and then absence; a valley where everything became confluence, plant, bird. Álvaro crossed the periphery of the city through an expressway, observing it from afar, from all possible angles, and then he went toward the Guardiola Hotel, where he asked for a room and ordered his usual whiskey as well as a pack of cigarettes.

The decision to go out was unpremeditated. The cold pushed him outside, and just like the first time he had been in the city, it invited him to take a walk in the winter gale. Once again Álvaro let his body guide him, knowing beforehand that at any moment he would arrive at the old house where he had seen Irena wrapped in an absurd silk dress approximately one year ago. When he was in front of the black iron gate, his hands pressed the buzzer and smoothed his hair. He waited. He waited without knowing what he would say, or even imagining what he was looking for.

"But Rolando, how good of you to come back." The woman had opened the gate a crack with excessive precaution, but as soon as she recognized him, she opened the door wide and embraced him. Álvaro, taken by surprise, let her do as she wished.

"It's wonderful you've come, really," the woman repeated with tears in her eyes, "your sister needs you so much. You can't imagine."

In effect, Álvaro couldn't imagine it. Still hugging him, the woman led Álvaro through a narrow hallway until once again she opened another door, a bigger one made of wood. Inside were the gold statuettes, the oil paintings, the lamps that radiated a wan, tenuous light, the Persian rugs, and the sofa upholstered in purple brocade where Álvaro had seen Irena make love with a man who was in a hurry. Suddenly full of sorrow he gazed across the space and became quiet.

"Hercules, isn't that so?" Someone inside him asked the question in the form of an affirmation.

And the woman nodded.

"He's getting worse, Rolando, that man's jealousy is suffocating her," she said with her half-shut eyes and pale lips.

At that moment, just before the woman began to speak again, a slow, deep, and terrible noise invaded the room. It was a tremor, a shaking of the earth. Soon, the rumble became more intense, and after what seemed an eternity, silence returned, a silence as loud as the noise itself.

"Antonia!" A cry came from another room.

Summoned, the woman excused herself and immediately ran out. The dust that the shaking left behind transformed the atmosphere. Álvaro barely managed to stand up with his energy depleted by fear, and as he tried to arrange some of the statues and other objects that had moved, he found the photograph that explained the mistaken identity. Irena and a man identical to her were embracing in front of a bay that seemed to him gray and icy. Undoubtedly it was Copenhagen. The image of the twins moved him.

"You look so much like her, don't you?" said Antonia as soon as she returned.

Álvaro turned, and with astonishment and pleasure, never before having felt so puzzled, he confirmed in a mirror that, in effect, his face and Irena's had a slight family resemblance. He hadn't noticed it before, but at this moment, he was grateful for the error. Because of it, not only had Antonia taken him into her confidence, she also shared stories that would have been difficult for him to imagine.

"Is everything OK?" asked Álvaro.

"Yes, young man, don't worry. My daughter gets very nervous when there are tremors, even one as mild as this one," she explained.

Then she offered him coffee and more conversation.

"That man is terrifying, Rolando," she continued her story. "When he's here—fortunately less and less often—he's angry all the time. He's always criticizing your sister and doesn't leave her alone: that she doesn't know how to cook, that she leaves glasses of water all over the house, that she doesn't rejoice in his successes or lick his wounds when he fails; that she doesn't dote on him. It's unbelievable. I sincerely do not know what Irena does to put up with him."

"She must be in love," Álvaro dared to guess. "Still," he added doubtfully.

Antonia looked at him as if through a fog, with a sadness that was difficult for her to hide.

"I don't think she does anymore, Rolando. But you're right; how she loved him!"

Antonia turned her face toward the corner of the room. "Imagine leaving behind her life in Copenhagen to come and shut herself up in a dump this size. Without any family. Without anything. Why did they let your sister do something like this?"

"Irena was already the legal age when everything happened, Antonia. Remember."

Someone inside Álvaro listed reasons in a firm and logical manner. Someone looked at the photograph of the twins with an odd, bitter, treacherous nostalgia. Someone was in pain.

"She must have been very much alone, I suppose. Perhaps it was a moment of madness," murmured Antonia with an absent-minded gaze between sips of coffee. "That's what happens to women who study a lot, isn't it?"

208

Álvaro smiled. Then he nodded in order to keep silent, just because. At any rate, Antonia wasn't paying attention to him anymore. She had shut herself up in an internal world full of stories that as she herself said could not be expressed in words. Suddenly the image of Hercules made Álvaro's blood boil and for the first time he was afraid for Irena and for himself. Abruptly, the memory of a winter afternoon in Copenhagen restored peace to him. Then, disconcerted, he realized that he had never been in Denmark. He needed a cigarette.

"I guess it's because of her daughter, don't you think? If he weren't hiding her, surely Irena would have already left, isn't that so, Rolando?"

Although the information startled him, he tried to maintain his composure. He nodded in silence, as if he accepted the validity of Antonia's opinions and then, nervously, he asked if he could smoke.

Antonia's weak and sorrowful tone echoed his, as she asked for a cigarette in turn.

"She's going to be four in December," she observed before lighting her cigarette. "He said he's keeping her abroad."

"Yes," muttered Álvaro.

The smoke from his cigarette rose in the air with the slow pace of sorrow. Álvaro felt an immense urge to get up and leave, but his unease prevented him from applying his energy. It was already past two in the morning when he finally decided to cross the wooden threshold and return to his hotel.

"Take care of yourself, Rolando. You never know what that man is capable of." She kissed him on each cheek, and without saying anything more, she closed the door before he had time to thank her.

When he got to his room he fell into a deep sleep. He was both tired and fed up. The illicit affairs of a normal man were surely more vulgar, but also less confusing. If it were only a matter of harboring hopes, of having his way with her on the nearest bed and letting himself go. It wasn't rocket science. Furthermore it happened all the time. A man had sex with a woman, while she made love with him. That was the thing, the whole point. Disgusted, Álvaro covered his head with the pillow and stopped thinking. Before completely shutting down his awareness, however, he remembered Antonia's error and he smiled wanly. Irena's twin. Her brother. A man with whom she had shared a winter afternoon facing the gray sky on a pier in Denmark. The man she trusted.

A dream he couldn't remember gnawed at the nape of his neck when he got up, took his customary bath, and had breakfast. He was uneasy; even inside the hotel room he turned his face from left to right as if someone were watching him from afar. He heard footsteps that stopped without warning, and voices that persisted inconsiderately. When he shut the door of his room he checked the pockets of his pants and his jacket with the feeling that he had forgotten something. He didn't find anything. He was getting ready to descend three flights of stairs when he saw two men dragging a gigantic black bag.

"Whose body is it?" he asked jokingly, suddenly in a good mood.

"Nobody knows."

The response left him speechless and made him tremble inside. He had never before been near a dead person. Still without reacting, he stood aside to let the men and their enormous bundle through. Contrary to what could be expected, Álvaro was hungry when he got to the restaurant. He wanted to fill his mouth with fruit, hot and spicy foods and festive colors. When his order came, he sniffed the coffee and food several times before ingesting them.

For his trip to the volcano he chose music by Sibelius. He drove carefully, probing his mood: sometimes he felt he was going to get there too late; at others, he felt like getting lost on purpose. The dilemma was resolved only when he observed the very white, high clouds in the sky: he'd go up the mountain, up the path, into the thin air. He had to see Irena. He had to confirm that she was real, that in some area of the world the forest existed, and within the forest, the cabin, and in the cabin the woman dressed in sky blue who was carrying something in her that belonged only to him. *Sirena*. When he left the highway behind to take the dirt road that would lead him to the cabin of his soulmate, Álvaro was smiling. The smile accompanied him while he walked under the pine trees and saw a flock of lambs. Then, when he opened the door of the cabin, the smile evaporated; he was aghast.

"But Irena, what happened to you?"

The woman was crouching in a corner of the house. She was hiding her face behind her knees, and from her matted hair emerged a pair of nervous arms in clumsy and syncopated movements. Her moans filled the atmosphere of decayed matter; it was something incomprehensible. Álvaro came close to her and when he did so, Irena tried to become even smaller.

"No," she said.

It seemed as if she had lost her mind.

"It's me, Irena. It's me."

The woman finally turned to look at him. Her face was crisscrossed by scarlet-colored scratches and bruises. Her lips, opened in furrows of fresh blood, pronounced his name while her swollen eyes tried to identify him.

"Rolando," she said and hugged him.

Then, she fainted or lost consciousness. At any rate, she closed her eyes and rested. The insistent bleating of a lamb reminded him that he was far from civilization.

211

With the help of his first aid kit, Álvaro was able to dress some of the wounds; but since Irena did not come to, he decided to take her to the nearest hospital. He wrapped her in a blanket and walked the stretch of path that separated them from his car. Breathing heavily but with his energy intact, undoubtedly because of the adrenaline, Álvaro managed to make out from afar the withered face of Ezequiel, the little man who, the year before, had helped them get out of that inhospitable place. Stretched out on the back seat, Irena looked like a bundle of bones, a flower shorn of its petals, a broken line.

"But she's a woman," Álvaro said to himself, "remember that she's a woman."

He drove as Irena had done before, at lunatic speed. The emergency guided him all the way to the hospital. When he arrived, a distracted doctor ordered X-rays, and after examining Irena, looked at him suspiciously.

"Are you her husband?"

"No, Doctor. I'm her brother," said Álvaro. "Her husband's name is Hercules."

"I see," said the doctor.

A couple of hours later, Álvaro found out that Irena had three broken ribs and was suffering from the secondary effects of a nervous breakdown. When the doctor suggested filing a complaint with the authorities, Álvaro hesitated. He had never been in a situation like this one. He didn't know exactly how big the enemy was; he didn't have the slightest idea of Irena's preferences; nor did he know if he should trust the police. The thought of notifying Antonia now passed through his mind, but Hercules's proximity made him afraid again. After thinking about it for a little while, he decided to bring Irena to Mexico City. He wouldn't be able to lodge her in the apartment on the thirteenth floor, but he thought of a room with big windows in the Sorrento. That way, far from the volcano and from Hercules, she would heal and he, her brother and lover and confidant, would be able to see her whenever he wanted during her convalescence. That night, while he slept in the bed next to Irena, the smell of disinfectant in the hospital produced another dream. Just like the one that had awakened him in the Guardiola Hotel, this dream had no name. He couldn't remember it.

It wasn't until Sunday that they returned to Mexico City. On the trip Irena was awake but stubbornly silent. She let herself be led around like an invalid or a little girl. At times she gave the impression that in reality nothing interested her very much, especially her life.

"Where are you taking me?" she asked when they crossed La Marquesa.

"To the Sorrento," answered Álvaro, looking at her from the corner of his eye, trying to put her in a good mood.

Irena made a face that didn't quite become a smile and afterward she fell asleep.

Without having agreed to, both gave the names of each other's siblings when they asked for a double room. Rolando and Sonia. Through the windows the city was a gathering of fireflies.

Taking advantage of Fuensanta's absence, Álvaro slept in Irena's room that night. Every so often when he looked at her, he'd wake her up to give her the medication and then he tucked her in once more. He didn't exactly know what kept him close to her, remembering and forgetting her with equal ease, but he supposed that it was something powerful.

"Perhaps you're my destiny, Irena," he whispered softly, so that no one would hear such a hackneyed phrase.

Then, with renewed vigor, he substituted it for another he imagined to be more exact:

"Maybe you're my fate."

This time he fell asleep.

The first week Irena spent in the Sorrento was marked by disorientation and confusion. Álvaro arrived everywhere late, and everywhere he seemed distracted and in a bad mood. Fuensanta constantly asked him, "What are you thinking about, Álvaro?" which added to his silent resentment.

"Leave me alone, Fuen. It's nothing," he managed to say with his mouth full of lies.

Then he'd go running to the hotel as if his life depended on it. It was obvious that Irena wasn't expecting him. By her sudden starts, her nervousness, by the way in which she chewed her nails, one knew she was expecting someone else. Hercules. The cruel man.

He asked her about him one Thursday afternoon, just before sundown. Irena sat down on the bed and cracked her knuckles.

"Do you really want to know?" she inquired before deciding to speak.

He could not help but be fascinated by the threat implicit in her question. Álvaro immediately responded that yes, he wanted to know.

"Hercules was so different, Álvaro," began Irena with her gaze fixed on a cold and distant place. When he knocked on my door the first time, he had the eyes of a lamb and the attitude of a needy person. He didn't know anyone else in Copenhagen who spoke Spanish and when he found out that I lived in the building, he turned up right away. Two or three months later everything changed. He had the ferocity of a wounded animal, and however much I tried, I couldn't get him out of my house. Or my life."

Irena fell silent. She turned to look at him and then, observing the intense colors of the sunset, continued: "I was pregnant."

The silence that followed was a long one, thin as a needle.

"And in love, I suppose," said Álvaro, encouraging her to go on.

"No, not in love. I've always been a woman of fragile loves, Álvaro," she said with a half smile on her face.

It was the first time he saw something like that since she arrived in Mexico City.

"He didn't love me anymore either, but Hercules is cruel. His lack of love turned into hate, and hate into this"—she pointed to the bruises on her face—"Do you believe me?" she interrupted herself.

"Why shouldn't I believe you?" asked Álvaro surprised.

"Hercules is like one of those characters in a horror novel," she continued without answering his question. "He's charming in public, but when he's alone he's powerless against his own bile. He produces it in enormous quantities. He gulps it down but he often chokes on it, and then he spits it out and dirties everything around him. I don't know," she said changing her tone to one full of compassion. "Perhaps he had an unhappy childhood."

Álvaro kissed her on the nape of her neck and lay down by her side. A cloud of melancholy was raining blue water inside the room.

"Or perhaps everything is due to his addiction," she added with affected carelessness. "Drugs put him very much inside himself, you know, where his worst self is."

Álvaro for the first time felt that his life was out of control. He couldn't endure Irena's confessions, although he himself had induced them with indiscrete questions and opportune comments. He had expected something else. A story of love with strong passions and inexplicable obsessions. A woman prepared to give up everything for a man, or perhaps the contrary. But it was nothing like that. Irena's was a story of "fragile loves." His disappointment was huge. The more he knew, the more uncomfortable he felt, the more out of place. And what if Hercules were to go looking for him to give him a good beating and take his wife back to the enchanted forest? Would it be worth it? He wasn't even sure anymore of his interest in Irena. He was surrounded by confusion, degradation, deterioration, decay. Irena was an ambiguous woman.

"You, on the other hand, have always been the man of my dreams," murmured Irena, as if she could read his mind.

It was as if Álvaro were seeing her through the lens of a very sunny day. He half shut his eyes and with incredulity repeated the phrase *I've always been her dream man.* The grammatical mingling of the sentences produced an emptiness in his stomach. For a moment he didn't know if he was the dream of a woman or the man who dreamed of a woman who was dreaming of a man dreaming of a woman. A linguistic vertigo forced him to close his eyes. When he opened them, he was in his bedroom, underneath the blankets, his right arm barely touching Fuensanta's shoulder. Around him the sun's morning rays were already shining.

That morning he had a phone call from Hercules Corvián. Just as his wife had done, he made an appointment with Álvaro to meet at the Siracusa at 4:15 that afternoon. In his voice there was not the slightest sign of doubt: he was sure that Engineer Diéguez, as he had called Álvaro, would come to the meeting.

"Antonia is right, you look a lot like Rolando," said Hercules by way of introduction.

Then he took off his hat of a bygone time, led him toward one of the tables in the back, and without asking Álvaro, ordered two whiskeys.

"Perhaps I am."

Someone inside him was playing with language, motivated by fear and desolation. Someone inside him observed Hercules with an almost feminine apprehension and unshakeable rancor. He would not let himself be defeated. He would not let Hercules defeat them. That man with a withered face and bony hands could do nothing against him, against her, or against reason.

"I'm going to tell you about it because I'm sure she filled your head with lies," he began.

A minute later and almost without transition, Álvaro found himself listening attentively to the story of Irena told through a mouth with thick lips and stained teeth.

"Irena is obsessed with the idea of being the victim of the whole world. Now it happens that I'm her executioner, isn't that so? Don't let her make a fool of you, Engineer Diéguez. About the beating, ask Ezequiel; and with respect to Copenhagen, remind her of the many humiliations she made me go through. She'd put me down all the time. How could someone with a doctorate in sick plants lower herself to be with a guy like me?"

The hate that came out of his mouth had no bounds. As he spoke without tolerating any kind of interruption, a fragility full of pointy edges seemed to break his puny body in two; but then, as his words continued to pierce the atmosphere with sharp arrows, the hardness of his gestures gave him the appearance of a commonplace, vulgar man.

"And surely she never told you about the times she beat me," continued Hercules, extinguishing a cigarette in a round ashtray with brusque movements and without paying attention to Alvaro's confusion and annoyance.

"My God, Hércules, don't be ridiculous. Everyone knows that when men make women mad, they react by trying to hit them, but they just don't know how," said Álvaro with a tone of boredom in his voice, and without really believing what he was hearing.

He felt as he did at that party where he remembered Irena, the party where a couple slung accusatory insinuations at each other until embarrassment forced them to leave. What was Hercules looking for by giving him his own version of the facts? To clear his name? To pass himself off as a good guy? He wouldn't be able to, thought Álvaro, and not because his version wasn't as valid as Irena's, but because the hate he emitted when he talked, and that filtered through each of his sentences, made his words suspect. Hercules was at a crossroads: the motivation which pushed him to fight on was the same that doomed him to failure. Without hate he could win allies, but without hate there was no point in tormenting his wife, the mother of his daughter, his partner. When he was preparing to leave, Álvaro could only look at him with compassion and disgust. He barely mumbled a couple of syllables by way of farewell, and left running in the direction of the Sorrento. He needed to see Irena. He needed to tell her that he was in agreement, that Hercules was in reality a cruel man, and that she was in danger. She had to leave her cabin, her enchanted forest, the cold of the Nevado. She had to go away however she could, return to that institute in Arizona perhaps; she had to save herself. She had to take care of herself, take her medications, stay well for their walks together, for the silly innocence they shared. Álvaro's mouth was full of words for Irena, but when he reached the room at the Sorrento, she had already left. *Don't kid yourself, Álvaro. I don't exist.*

Three days later, while Álvaro was still torturing himself trying to decide between searching for Irena and forgetting her forever, Fuensanta informed him that she was pregnant. At that moment his dilemma was resolved with the immediate initiation of a new life. A life marked by the warmth of another, a life without cold. A life without Irena.

Álvaro was happy. When he looked at himself discreetly in the mirrors of his house, a pride that was real, though cautious, crossed his face. He felt satisfaction. He had a job that he not only enjoyed, but that allowed him to live with decorum and more. A stable and lasting affection joined him to his wife. He had Mariano, a son almost two years old in whose eyes he found inexhaustible quantities of peace and hope. He had friends, books into which he could delve alone, and favorite cinemas. He had a routine which steered him through the chaos of everyday life. He had a future, hundreds of them. At thirty-three, Álvaro had attained everything he had dreamed of at fourteen, perhaps even more. At the age of Christ, he could not find any reason to complain about life, while he did indeed have much to be grateful for. Álvaro knew this. It was enough for him to observe the nearness of Fuensanta and Mariano to verify that he was a whole man.

During Mariano's second birthday party, however, a strange sensation transformed the tranquility of his new life. It was an old, fuzzy, wounded feeling. It had been consuming him for a long time until, weak, pale, and moribund, but still alive, it reached his feet. The feeling which made him stand still and hesitate came to him from within the pages of a book. It was *Sirens of the Highlands*, the most recent book by Nélida Cruz, the anthropologist in whose house he had witnessed the embarrassing fight of an incompatible married couple.

"Thank you, Nélida," said Álvaro upon receiving it.

The book was a precious object. The care taken with the edition was noticeable not only in the quality of the paper and the font, but also, and perhaps in particular, on the front cover: an oil painting by a local artist in which beings that seemed only half human looked at the reader with eyes full of an almost divine sadness. Álvaro observed the painting for a couple of minutes, with a curiosity that seemed to belong to someone else. Then, when he recognized her, he placed the book on the nearest table without saying a word. He was sure that one of the faces was Irena's. Until that moment he hadn't thought about her for three years.

"What are you thinking about, Álvaro?" Fuensanta asked when Mariano was sleeping in his room and the dishes, slices of birthday cake, and deflated balloons filled the apartment with melancholy.

"Nothing, Fuen," he answered with an unaccustomed meekness in his voice.

Then, without saying a word, he put his arm around her waist, drawing her toward him, and as he observed Nélida's book from the corner of his eye, he held her close to him for a long time. As soon as Fuensanta went to sleep, Álvaro retrieved the book and began to read it in one of the armchairs in the living room. He skipped the first chapter, where Nélida showed off her theoretical knowledge by quoting Geertz, Bakhtin, and Taussig with a prolixity that bordered on the irritating. Nor did he read a chapter where the anthropologist described in detail her method of gathering data. He skimmed through a long historical section where sirens of the whole world and from every period appeared and disappeared at will. Álvaro's attention was drawn to a short chapter near the end of the book, in which the author tried to describe, without much success, the story of a tiny siren which hovered around the Lagoons of the Sun and the Moon in the crater of the Nevado of Toluca, the dead volcano. While he read hurriedly, a chill ran up and down his spine. He stopped. He read once more.

As we have seen, the stories of mermaids of the highlands follow a more or less regular pattern. Among all of them, however, there is one that stands out both for the physical characteristics attributed to the said mermaid, as well as the faculties in which she takes pride. This legend has its origin in the ranches near Raíces, especially those nearest the crater. It involves a mermaid with sky-blue skin and very small physical proportions which vary according to the informant. Thus, the siren of the volcano is at times as small as a hand, and at others, as big as a local deer. In neither of the two examples does she manifest human dimensions. In contrast to the traditional Chanclana, whose principal faculty is to attract and destroy men, the sky-blue siren is timid and hides from others while taking on human guises. When men come upon her the dénouement is always fatal, although not immediate. It is said that on seeing her, men find something inside themselves—certain gestures, inclinations, thoughts, perhaps—whose fascination leads them, eventually, to madness. Her malignant work sometimes takes months, and, more frequently, whole years to produce effects, but these effects are inescapable.

Álvaro closed the book, and shaking his head, went to the bedroom where Fuensanta's warm and relaxed body awaited him. He took his clothes off, put on his pajamas, brushed his teeth and, finally, slipped under the covers. When he closed his eyes, the vision of a gray plain kept him awake. It was the North Sea, immobile and stark. At three in the morning he decided to get up. He went to the kitchen to prepare some tea, and observing the tops of the trees from the thirteenth floor, he pronounced Irena's name for the first time in a long while. He was concerned about her fate. He wondered about the three ribs that in all certainty had been broken by Hercules. Then, he cursed himself with a growing sense of guilt. He thought he had behaved like an imbecile, abandoning her at the moment when she needed him most, but then he remembered that it had been she who had disappeared without a trace. The feelings she provoked were confused and contradictory. Besides, he had had good reasons for his forgetfulness—the birth of his son. When Álvaro finally returned to bed, a light and uncomfortable sleep pervaded him. When he awoke his bones ached.

Two days later the perfect excuse to undertake a return to Toluca came: the publishing house which had produced Nélida Cruz's book was organizing a presentation in the city's cultural center, and the author invited them to attend. Fuensanta accepted immediately and Álvaro, without visible eagerness on his face, did the same. Suddenly memories pursued him. He tried to scare them away with his son's smile, but it was all useless. First came a feeling of cold, and then, the wan light of the highlands, the pine trees, the dirt path, the cabin, a lamb and its horrendous bleating. Then Hercules's face, framed by the walls of the Siracusa, appeared in all its crudeness. He tried to stop the memories, but by then he couldn't do anything. He was in another place and it was a lost cause. Álvaro knew that he had a secret that bore the name of a woman, and he also knew that the fact of having it upset him. Furthermore, that irritation was accompanied by fear. And if he found her again? And if *doña* Antonia ran into him on the street and called him Rolando? And if he came upon Irena in Hercules's arms? What if he didn't find her? Álvaro was forced to smile and recognize that he lacked answers to any question related to Irena.

They started out early, before the traffic drove the city insane, but after the sun came up. Fuensanta was in a good mood, humming to popular songs on the radio and observing Mariano's face from time to time. Just like Álvaro, she considered herself a whole and happy woman. When they were approaching the highest city and were already on the boulevard bordered by willows, Fuensanta's attitude changed.

"We came to this city a few years ago, do you remember, Álvaro?" she said, looking at him from the corner of her eye, as if it had just come to her mind.

"Yes, a few years ago, Fuen," mumbled Álvaro, doubtful that Fuensanta could have ever forgotten the trip they had taken so that he could enjoy the cold for a few hours.

Then they were silent and within that silence they crossed the city and left it behind. Without consulting her, Álvaro had decided to go up the mountain, up into the thin air, toward the foothills of the volcano. They crossed abandoned ranches, cornfields, barren slopes. They observed the gray, unreachable clouds. They counted the pines and the oak trees. Álvaro left the highway behind, took the dirt road, and soon they found themselves surrounded by different shades of green. They were in the enchanted forest. With Mariano in his arms, Álvaro walked up and down the slope with an unaccustomed hurry, a hurry that accelerated his breathing, making it almost impossible. Even then, he didn't stop until he glimpsed the cabin where, just a few years before, they had spent the night in Irena's presence. The disappointment on his face was immediate and obvious. The cabin which he remembered as picturesque and friendly was now an accumulation of discolored and badly arranged wooden boards. Surrounded by other little shacks of the same type, Irena's cabin was pathetic.

"Álvaro!"

He didn't notice Fuensanta's shout. Álvaro continued walking toward the place without listening or seeing, without feeling anything other than a strong expectation. When he reached the door, some children opened it from the inside, and without heeding him, ran around him as if playing an ancient game. They were dark-complexioned children with their cheeks red on account of the cold and the dry air, children with an easy laugh and unfamiliar faces, children wearing huaraches and thick sweaters of coarse wool or ponchos that were too big. The children's voices, mixed with the lambs' bleating, created disorder, a noise that irritated the senses. Álvaro continued on his way. He crossed the threshold of the door and although the darkness prevented him at first, he tried to see what he had seen in the past: a cabin like the lit-up interior of a walnut. Instead, he encountered the wrinkled faces of two men and a woman who were exchanging muffled murmurs while they drank some hot potion in clay mugs. There were no books, no fireplace, no colorful textiles on the wall, no candles.

"What can I do for you?" asked one of the men with some hostility and without getting up from his chair.

Álvaro was about to answer when the woman came closer, took his face between her rough hands, and began to cry with something like sadness.

"But it's you, Rolando, how late you've come, how late this time, young man."

It was an older Antonia, with the same voice of surprise and an almost unrecognizable face. It seemed as if she had aged a hundred years.

"Don't look at me like that. It happens to everyone. Don't be afraid."

Certainly Álvaro was afraid. Suddenly he became aware that he was carrying his son and that he didn't have the slightest idea of where Fuensanta was. Furthermore, he was surrounded by ragged children, monosyllabic elders, and dirty lambs, inside a hut that could perhaps protect them from something but definitely not the cold; a hut that in addition did not open up in welcome but, on the contrary, closed itself, rejecting him.

"Irena," he managed to stammer, "Irena."

Suddenly, the name seemed to him unbearable; his presence there, ridiculous. Antonia looked at him calmly, took him by the arm and made him sit down at the table. Her movements were so slow that they seemed to him eternal. By then accustomed to the dim light, Álvaro recognized Hercules's face in a large photograph which covered one of the windows of the place. It was the face of a smiling man under which a motto in red and green letters was inscribed: "I'm a friend of the *Mexiquenses*." It seemed to be part of a political campaign and to belong to a different era.

"You're late, young man," repeated the old woman as she served him hot coffee in another clay mug. "I warned you that your sister needed you; I told you many times, Rolando."

Recrimination filled her voice and made her tremble with something like a mixture of passion and sorrow. Disturbed by the accusation, Álvaro was about to confess that he wasn't Rolando, but at that moment Mariano extracted himself from his arms and ran toward the group of children that were still playing around the cabin. His concern forced him to stand up, but one of the men held him by the arm with the strength of a boy of twenty.

"Nothing's going to happen to him. Let him play with his friends," said the man in a tone of command.

Then, he stationed himself in the doorway in a threatening position. Little by little, as Álvaro began to identify Mariano's voice among the other children's voices, he became calm.

"Why did you come?"

The question the second man was asking him was full of the same unfriendliness and the same recrimination he had heard before.

"I don't know," Álvaro said after thinking about it for a while. "Really, I don't know."

Then he collapsed. The sincerity of his response won him the sympathy of the elderly people seated around Irena's table. Their gaze, which had been rude earlier, settled with compassion on his back.

"Losing a sister is the worst thing that can happen to somebody," murmured Antonia in a barely audible tone. "Especially when they were the only children and twins, besides."

While they all nodded in silence, Álvaro was filled with sorrow and terror. Sorrow for the sister he had lost without even knowing it, and terror because the confusion of identities was going so far that it was confusing even him.

"I'm not Rolando," he affirmed suddenly, thinking of Sonia, his real sister.

"Oh, son," answered the woman, placing his hands in between hers, "it's always the same. When the pain is so great, you always wish you're not who you are."

The tone of understanding ingrained in her voice was the sign of her age, her gray hair and long striated wrinkles. Álvaro started up from his seat.

"No, Antonia, I'm really not Rolando," he repeated with more anguish than firmness in his voice.

"And I'm not Antonia," murmured the woman in a joking tone, trying to show him the extent of his foolishness.

Convinced that the conversation was useless, Álvaro continued to stand and looked through the windows. In the distance, the enchanted forest was still immobile, indestructible, crowned by large gray clouds. Nearby, the group of children was running as if the natural shape of the world was round. He recognized Mariano among them, and then, he discovered that holding the boy's hand was a little girl whose face he forgot and remembered with astonishing ease.

"Who is she?" he asked the old people while he pointed to a slim girl with chestnut-colored hair who it seemed was taking care of his son.

"Little Mariana has always liked children, isn't that so?" they remarked among themselves as if in reality nobody had asked them anything.

Álvaro went out of the cabin and toward his son with the intention of rescuing him from an undefined but imminent danger.

"Uncle Rolando," the little girl shouted at the same time that she stretched out her arms to him.

Álvaro couldn't avoid opening his own arms wide to receive her in them. Then, no longer knowing how to act or what to do, he surrendered to the ambiguities.

"Come," said Mariana taking his left hand.

He followed her with his son in his arms. The girl, who was dressed in brown corduroy overalls and work boots, guided them with confident steps through the pine trees and solitary paths full of sharp-pointed rocks. They went up the mountain, into the thin air, until they left the forest behind. When they did that, they penetrated the amorphous body of a low-lying cloud. Then, to his complete surprise, they found themselves in front of the lagoons formed by the water in the volcano's crater. The landscape surrounding them was desertlike, useless land. Álvaro was tired but the timeless beauty of the place eased his breathing. Mariano, asleep in his arms, was not able to observe the tense stillness of the waters, the delicateness of the air, the meager warmth of the sunlight that filtered through the cluster of gray clouds.

"My mother went away in that direction," Mariana announced to him as she looked toward the lagoons.

There was no sadness in her gaze. In her eyes, the green color associated with hope radiated from her translucent pupils. She kept quiet for a moment while throwing little white stones toward the Lagoon of the Sun, and then, as if the trek hadn't required any effort, she turned to look at him to indicate that they should return. This time Álvaro didn't obey her. He took off his jacket to cover his son's body and sat down in the same spot where he was standing.

"I can't go on anymore," he told the girl with complete honesty.

"That's what my mama always used to say," answered Mariana, who without any premeditation turned her back to him and began the walk back.

Observing the growing distance between them Álvaro suddenly understood everything that had happened and knew what he had to do. He called to her. He shouted her name and asked her to wait for him. Then, he took her hand and guided her down the slope with a firmness and wisdom that he was just discovering. Slowly, stopping here and there to pronounce the names of some plants, Álvaro walked with his two children until he arrived at the cabin. There, surrounded by the old people, the lambs and the other children, Fuensanta was waiting for them with a look of distress and her muscles tensed. When she glimpsed them in the distance, the joy of seeing them return safe and sound mattered more than her anger. She ran to hug them.

"Let's get out of this place, Álvaro," she whispered in his ear. "Everything is cursed," she added while she looked around her, encompassing it all within a long and watery look.

Álvaro obeyed. He took his son in his arms, and, carefully, with the speed of someone who is trying to elude death, he began the walk back to the car. He didn't say good-bye; he didn't turn around, and while he advanced hurriedly, he didn't hear anything except his agitated breathing. When he saw the car in the distance, it occurred to him that it was a matter of his own personal salvation. Then, with the same nervous speed, he opened the doors and awaited Fuensanta's prompt arrival. The syncopated movement of their bodies drove him crazy: he didn't know what he was seeing, or what exactly to pay attention to. A knee. A forearm. The heel of a shoe. An eye. Two. They had to leave immediately. As soon as he heard the door slam, he turned on the engine and stepped on the accelerator. It wasn't until a couple of miles later that, looking at the rearview mirror out of the corner of his eye, he realized Mariana was in the back seat.

"And what are you doing here?" asked Fuensanta in amazement, noticing her at the same time.

228

"My mama told me that one day you'd come for me," answered Mariana in a terse and natural voice, looking at Álvaro in the rearview mirror. "She said that you had always been the man of her dreams," she added, looking at the landscape through the windows, no longer paying attention to them.

Fuensanta repeated the last sentence through her teeth and kept quiet. Álvaro did the same. Mariano, sleeping in his car seat, contributed to the gathering silence. Mariana didn't say another word. The volcano covered with snow watched them from afar.

The situation, like all those created directly or indirectly by Irena, was absurd. Álvaro couldn't understand what a girl with a serious expression, who looked out with a weary gaze that did not correspond to her age, was doing in his car. He didn't know what explanation he would give Fuensanta when, no longer surrounded by the children, they sat down at the table to talk. Nor did he know who Irena was or had been. Above all, he didn't know who the dream man was. As they left behind the enchanted forest, the only thing that Álvaro could do was look out of the corner of his eye at the rearview mirror, hoping with all his heart that he would not find Mariana's face. However, that face continued to be there every time that his nervousness or incredulity forced him to spy on the back seat of the car. Mariana, Mariana Corvián. What would he tell Fuensanta? What would he keep quiet? Within that silence, while the city came closer with its curved spinal cord of lights, Álvaro once again spelled out the word "absurd." Everything, without a doubt, was absurd.

Fuensanta didn't break her silence when they got back to the apartment. Without saying a word, she prepared to feed her son while she showed Mariana where the towels and the bathroom were. When, freshly bathed, the little girl was ready for supper, Fuensanta placed a bowl of cereal on the table, which the child ate without appetite. Then after both children were fed, Fuensanta led them to the bedroom where she tucked them in, turned off the light, and said good night. Afterward, she went to the balcony where Álvaro was waiting for her with a contrite expression. Fuensanta observed her husband with a questioning look, but not with distrust. She knew him well. She knew that Álvaro was not the kind of man who suffered from romantic passions or single-minded obsessions. She had faith in him.

"So," she said, bringing a chair closer and placing a bottle of tequila and two glasses on the little table, and asking him, to his complete surprise, for a cigarette.

"None of this has a logical explanation, Fuensanta," murmured Álvaro.

"I know," she answered. "Or so I imagine," she corrected herself.

The human silence that formed between them was voluminous and uncomfortable. But the night of the city crept up on them, with a multitude of disorganized noises that were difficult to identify. Without saying a word, they clinked glasses for the first time.

"Mariana is the daughter of a cruel man and a timid siren," began Álvaro with an ironic smile half-outlined on his face. "Mariana is the daughter of Irena, Fuen. Do you remember her?"

Fuensanta remembered. She had barely heard the name when she wrinkled her nose, and with a couple of weary gestures asked Álvaro for the lighter. Then, after lighting her cigarette, she went to the wrought iron railing and rested her arms on it.

"Her father is, or was, a shady sort who it seems had taken her abroad, perhaps to Copenhagen, without Irena's permission." Someone inside him knew stories that he personally was unfamiliar with, and then handed out explanations with unheard-of aplomb. "It seems that Hércules is, or was, a local politician."

"Hercules Corvián? The candidate?" The incredulity on Fuensanta's face was genuine.

"Do you know him?"

"Everyone knows him, Álvaro. He's the worst kind, connected to narcotics trafficking it seems," she said exasperatedly and then, without transition, she said loudly, "What can a man like that and the doctor in sick plants have in common?"

"Violence," said Álvaro immediately, surprising even himself.

Then, he told his wife about the hospital incident, omitting Irena's stay in the Sorrento.

"How could a woman like that, with all those words in her mouth, allow herself to be beaten up by a jerk like Corvián? No, Álvaro, it's too hard to comprehend," concluded Fuensanta, who at this juncture was more interested in the story itself than in the way Álvaro had found out about it. "Didn't you ever see him in those TV ads? A guy with no class, with his outmoded hat and the look of a shameless, down-and-out bum. It's horrible."

Álvaro was astonished by his own ignorance. Never in his life had he seen the ads that his wife was referring to, but all her descriptions corresponded to the man whom he had once met in the Siracusa. In his confusion, they clinked their glasses a second time.

"I think they met in Copenhagen but I don't know anything else."

"She must have gone crazy. Isn't that what tends to happen to women who study a lot?"

Without meaning to, Fuensanta was repeating Antonia's words. Then, again without any transition, she pressed him to continue:

"And about Mariana, how did you meet the girl?"

"Like you, Fuen. I met her today."

The sincerity of his voice won over his wife's sympathy. She came closer to him.

"She doesn't act like a child, Álvaro, did you notice that?" she said in a murmur. "She looks at you like a grown-up; she behaves like someone much older."

Álvaro nodded in complete agreement.

"I think Mariana has witnessed some terrible things in her life, Fuen," Álvaro said, as he narrated his trek toward the volcano's crater: the Lagoon of the Sun, the Lagoon of the Moon; *My mother went away in that direction*, the black water, the cold wind, the clouds where gray exploded in a thousand tonalities and textures, a still life. "I don't know what we're going to do with her," he concluded with a question mark in one eye and a plea in the other.

Fuensanta kept silent and looked out at the night, indicating she had understood. The decision would be hers and hers alone. The tequila on her tongue awakened her senses.

"At the beginning I thought that Irena was a friendly woman, Álvaro," murmured Fuensanta, "but her way of repeating the names of plants wasn't normal, was it? It couldn't be. Did you also notice that she didn't feel the cold?"

Fuensanta asked and answered her questions simultaneously. Rather than conversing, she seemed to be elaborating a monologue that had been deferred for a long time.

"I should throw a jealous tantrum, shouldn't I?" she went on. "I should ask you where this happened, how you found out about it, when, and at what time. But Irena wasn't a woman who could provoke jealousy in another, Álvaro. Compassion, pity, perhaps: something like that."

Fuensanta was silent again while she searched for the exact words, the most precise terms, but she couldn't find them.

"Irena wasn't looking for love. You could tell that from a mile away, Álvaro. She wanted something else. Protection perhaps. Maybe protection from herself. A way to leave."

"She found it," he muttered, observing his wife's faraway eyes.

"Her dream man." Fuensanta repeated the words several times, as if hypnotized. "How curious, Álvaro, what a turn of phrase. Did I ever tell you that I also came to think that a woman had dreamed you up for me? Yes, don't laugh"—she gave his shoulder a gentle push and took another sip of tequila—"I always thought that you were the dream of a feverish woman who in her hurry forgot you on the pavement where I later found you by chance, just like you find your blessings. There's no better way to describe what I feel for you."

Álvaro looked at her with amazement, gratitude, and incredulity. Fuensanta had never told him anything like that in her whole life. Not even in the steamiest moments of their relationship, not even at the beginning, when everything had been enchantment and seduction, had she been prey to clumsy sentiments or passionate dramas. Just as she had said at that party where the ill-suited couple had fought in secret, Fuensanta was in reality a man. Sure of herself, fulfilled in her daily activities, contained in the expression of her emotions, at peace with her surroundings. And now this slightly tipsy woman who smoked cigarettes while she was confessing to him a love greater than he had ever imagined, seemed totally unfamiliar. Still dazed, he raised the glass of tequila to his lips, without losing sight of her: a hitherto unheard-of face, an unrecognizable expression, a hidden woman suddenly revealed that night. He liked what he saw. All of a sudden he wanted to see her like that for the rest of his life. Suddenly he was sure that he was dreaming. Then, as the two struggled to look each other in the eye, a pale light illuminated the scene on the balcony. Both of them turned their faces toward the interior of the apartment, and with surprise they discovered the figure of Mariana who was watching them from behind the armchair in the living room. The girl was standing, immobile. A wounded statue. They were afraid and felt like running away. Scantily clad in a sky-blue nightgown, Mariana seemed to be a beacon that offered its light to a perfectly calm ocean. A timid siren. Through her big green eyes, another woman illuminated the couple's silhouette.

He was a man who dreamed.

She was too.

Contributor Notes

Sulaiman Addonia is an Eritrean-Ethiopian-British novelist. His first novel, *The Consequences of Love*, shortlisted for the Commonwealth Writers' Prize, was translated into more than twenty languages. *Silence Is My Mother Tongue*, his second, was longlisted for the 2019 Orwell Prize for Political Fiction. He currently lives in Brussels where he has launched a creative writing academy for refugees and asylum seekers, and has founded the Asmara-Addis Literary Festival (In Exile), and co-founded with Specimen Press a new literary prize, To Speak Europe in Different Languages, honoring hybrid and collective writing.

Jakuta Alikavazovic is a French writer of Bosnian and Montenegrin origins. Her debut novel, *Corps volatils*, won the Prix Goncourt in 2008 for Best First Novel. She has translated into French works by Ben Lerner, David Foster Wallace, and Anna Burns. She lives in Paris and writes a regular column for the daily newspaper *Libération. Night as It Falls* is her first book published in English.

Julia Alvarez is the author of six novels, three books of nonfiction, three collections of poetry, and twelve books for children and young adults. *In the Time of the Butterflies*, with over a million copies in print, was selected by the National Endowment for the Arts for its national Big Read program, and in 2013 President Obama awarded Alvarez the National Medal of Arts. *Afterlife*, a new novel, and *Already a Butterfly*, a new picture book for young readers, were published in 2020.

Elizabeth Ayre is a writer based in New York City. She is currently attending the creative writing MFA program at New York University. This is her first publication.

Rick Bass, the author of thirty books, won the Story Prize for his collection *For a Little While* and was a finalist for the National Book Critics Circle Award for his memoir *Why I Came West*. His most recent book is *Fortunate Son: Selected Essays from the Lone Star State*. His work, which has appeared in the *New Yorker*, *The Atlantic*, *Esquire*, and the *Paris Review*, among many other publications, and has been anthologized numerous times in *The Best American Short Stories*, has also won multiple O. Henry Awards and Pushcart Prizes, as well as NEA and Guggenheim fellowships. Bass lives in Montana's Yaak Valley, where he is a founding board member of the Yaak Valley Forest Council.

Lana Bastašić is a Yugoslav-born writer. Her first novel, *Catch the Rabbit*, won the European Union Prize in Literature in 2020 and was published in English in 2021. *Mliječni zubi* (*Milk Teeth*), a collection of short stories, was published in Serbo-Croatian in 2020.

Joshua Bennett is the Mellon Assistant Professor of English and Creative Writing at Dartmouth College. He is the author of three books of poetry and criticism: *The Sobbing School*, winner of the National Poetry Series and a finalist for an NAACP Image

Award; *Owed*; and *Being Property Once Myself*, winner of the Thomas J. Wilson Memorial Prize. Bennett's writing has been published in *Best American Poetry*, the *New York Times*, the *Paris Review*, *Poetry*, and elsewhere. He has received fellowships from the National Endowment for the Arts, the Ford Foundation, MIT, and the Society of Fellows at Harvard University. His first work of narrative nonfiction, *Spoken Word: A Cultural History*, is forthcoming from Knopf.

Julia Cimafiejeva is a Belarusian poet and the author of three poetry collections. Her work has been translated into many languages. Cimafiejeva has translated and published several books of children's literature from Norwegian. Her diary of the post-election state violence and peaceful resistance in Belarus came out from Swedish publisher Norstedts in 2020. Born in the village of Spiaryzhzha in the south of Belarus, she lives in Minsk.

Sandra Cisneros is a poet, short story writer, novelist, essayist, and visual artist whose work explores the lives of Mexicans and Mexican-Americans. Her numerous awards include a MacArthur Fellowship, the National Medal of Arts, a Ford Foundation Art of Change Fellowship, and the PEN/Nabokov Award for Achievement in International Literature. Her novel *The House on Mango Street*, which has sold over six million copies and been translated into over twenty-five languages, is considered a classic. A new book, *Martita, I Remember You/Martita, te recuerdo*, will be published in 2021.

Linda Coverdale has a PhD in French Studies and has translated over eighty books. A Chevalier de l'Ordre des Arts et des Lettres, she has won many prizes, including the International IMPAC Dublin Literary Award and several Scott Moncrieff and French-American Foundation translation prizes. She lives in Brooklyn, NY.

Kamel Daoud is an Algerian journalist based in Oran, where he writes for the *Quotidien d'Oran*, the third largest French-language Algerian newspaper. He contributes a weekly column to *Le Point*, and his articles have appeared in *Libération*, *Le Monde*, *Courrier International*, and are regularly reprinted around the world. A finalist for the Prix Goncourt, *The Meursault Investigation* won the Prix François Mauriac and the Prix des Cinq Continents de la Francophonie. Rights to the novel have been sold in twenty countries. His latest novel is *Zabor, or The Psalms*.

Christy NaMee Eriksen is a multidisciplinary poet, teaching artist, and organizer living in Juneau, Alaska. Her work has appeared at The Loft Literary Center in Minneapolis, The Roundhouse in London, and the anthologies *Revolutionary Mothering: Love on the Front Lines* and *The World I Leave You: Asian American Poets on Faith & Spirit.* She is a three-time Rasmuson Foundation award recipient and a 2020 Kundiman fellow.

Author, translator, critic, **Cristina Rivera Garza**'s recent publications include *Grieving: Dispatches from a Wounded Country,* which was named a finalist for the National Book Critics Circle Award in criticism; *The Restless Dead: Necrowriting and Disappropriation*; *La Castañeda Insane Asylum: Narratives of Pain from Modern Mexico*; and *Autobiografía del algodón*. She is Distinguished Professor and founder of the PhD Program in Creative Writing in Spanish at the University of Houston, Department of Hispanic Studies and a MacArthur Fellow of 2020.

Francisca González-Arias has taught Spanish and courses on literature by Spanish and Latin American women writers for many years. Among her translations are works by Soledad Puértolas and Cristina Rivera Garza. She also translates from English to Spanish, most recently selected poems of Emily Dickinson. She lives in Cambridge, Massachusetts.

Lauren Groff is the author of three novels, *The Monsters of Templeton*, *Arcadia*, and *Fates and Furies*, and the short story collections *Delicate Edible Birds* and *Florida*. She has won the Story Prize, has been a finalist for the National Book Critics Circle Award and the *Los Angeles Times* Book Prize, and has twice been a finalist for the National Book Award. She was a Guggenheim fellow and named one of *Granta* magazine's 2017 Best of Young American Novelists. Her work has been published in thirty languages. Her fourth novel, *Matrix*, was published September 2021.

Celia Hawkesworth taught Serbian, Croatian, and Bosnian language and literature at the School of Slavonic and East European Studies, University of London, from 1971 to 2002. Since retiring she has been working as a freelance translator. She began translating fiction in the 1960s, and to date has published translations of some forty titles.

Aleksandar Hemon is the author of *The Question of Bruno*, *Nowhere Man*, *The Lazarus Project*, *Love and Obstacles*, *The Making of Zombie Wars*, *The Book of My Lives*, and *My Parents: An Introduction/This Does Not Belong to You*. He is working on his next novel, tentatively titled "The World and All That It Holds," as well as a work of nonfiction, *How Did You Get Here?: Tales of Displacement*, that was the recipient a PEN/Jean Stein Grant for Literary Oral History in 2017. Hemon is the winner of the 2020 John Dos Passos Prize. He cowrote the script for *The Matrix 4* with David Mitchell and Lana Wachowski.

Kyle Dillon Hertz received his MFA from New York University, where he received a Writer in the Public Schools Fellowship. He's at work on a novel. Find him on Instagram: @kyledillonhertz.

Rickey Laurentiis was raised in New Orleans, Louisiana, to love the dark. *Boy with Thorn*, their debut book, won the Cave Canem Poetry Prize, the Levis Reading Prize, and was a finalist for the Kate Tufts Discovery Award. Other honors include fellowships from the Lannan Literary Foundation, the National Endowment for the Arts, the Poetry Foundation, the Whiting Foundation, and the Center for African American Poetry and Poetics at the University of Pittsburgh.

Uladzimir Liankievič is a poet, translator, and musician. His debut award-winning poetry collection came out in 2014. He has been a part of several successful musical projects. In the fall of 2020, he was detained twice by the authoritarian regime in Belarus and served two sentences. He lives in Minsk.

Megan McDowell is an award-winning translator who has translated many of the most important Latin American writers working today, including Samanta Schweblin, Alejandro Zambra, Mariana Enriquez, and Lina Meruane. She is from Kentucky and lives in Santiago, Chile.

Lina Meruane is the award-winning Chilean author of *Nervous System* and *Seeing Red*. She has received grants from the Guggenheim Foundation and the National Endowment for the Arts, and was a DAAD Writer in Residence in Berlin. She teaches at New York University.

Lina Mounzer is a writer and translator living in Beirut. Her work has appeared in the *New York Times*, the *Paris Review*, *1843*, *Literary Hub*, and *Bidoun*, as well as in *Hikayat: Short Stories by Lebanese Women* and *Tales of Two Planets*, an anthology of writing on climate change and inequality.

Valzhyna Mort is the author of *Factory of Tears*, *Collected Body*, and mostly recently, *Music for the Dead and Resurrected*, which has been named one of the Best Poetry Books of 2020 by the *New York Times* and NPR. Mort is a recipient of fellowships from the National Endowment for the Arts, the Lannan Foundation, and the Amy Clampitt Fund. Her work has appeared in the *New Yorker*, the *New York Times*, *Best American Poetry*, *Poetry*, *Granta*, and *Poetry Review*, among many other publications. Born in Minsk, Belarus, she writes in English and Belarusian.

Sayaka Murata is the author of many books, including *Convenience Store Woman*, winner of Japan's most prestigious literary award, the Akutagawa Prize. Her latest novel to be translated into English is *Earthlings*. Murata was chosen for inclusion in *Freeman's: The Future of New Writing*, and was a *Vogue Japan* Woman of the Year.

Yoko Ogawa has written more than twenty works of fiction and nonfiction. Her fiction has appeared in the *New Yorker*, *Zoetrope*, and *A Public Space*. She has received every major Japanese literary prize and was a finalist for the National Book Award in 2019.

Siarhiej Prylucki was born in Brest, Belarus, and has lived in Ukraine since 2008. He is the author of five books of poetry and two books of prose. His work has been honored with several awards and fellowships, including being long-listed for the Jerzy Giedroyc Prize for the best book of the year.

Zahia Rahmani is one of France's leading art historians and writers of fiction, memoir, and cultural criticism. She is the author of a literary trilogy dedicated to contemporary figures of so-called banished people: *Moze* (2003); *"Muslim": A Novel ("Musulman" roman*, 2005); and *France, Story of a Childhood (France, récit d'une enfance*, 2006). The French Ministry of Culture named Rahmani Chevalier of Arts and Letters. As an art historian, Rahmani curated *Made in Algeria: Généalogie d'un territoire*, a large exhibition of colonial cartography, visual culture, and contemporary art at the Museum of European and Mediterranean Civilizations (MuCEM), Marseille, in 2016. The essay "Algeria: Held in Reserve" comes from the catalogue of that exhibition. Rahmani is currently curating the traveling exhibition *Seismography of Struggle: Towards a Global History of Critical and Cultural Journals*.

Yasmine El Rashidi is an Egyptian writer. She is the author of *The Battle for Egypt: Dispatches from the Revolution* and *Chronicle of a Last Summer: A Novel of Egypt*. She writes on politics and culture for the *New York Review of Books*, and is an editor of the Middle East arts and culture journal *Bidoun*. She lives in Cairo.

Matt Reeck is an American translator, poet, and scholar. He won the 2020 Albertine Prize for his translation of Zahia Rahmani's *"Muslim": A Novel*. He has won fellowships from the Fulbright Foundation, the National Endowment for the Arts, the PEN/Heim Translation Fund, and during Spring 2021, he served as Princeton

University's Translator in Residence. He has published seven translations from the French, Urdu, and Hindi.

Dmitry Rubin was born in the village of Sachanyaty in the southwest of Belarus. He writes poetry and short stories and is a columnist for several literary publications. His first book of short prose will come out from Knihazbor Press in Minsk once the state violence against the Belarusian literary community stops.

Damion Searls translates from French, German, Norwegian, and Dutch, and is the author of a book of short stories, a history of the Rorschach test, and *The Philosophy of Translation* (forthcoming). He has received Guggenheim, Cullman Center, and NEA fellowships, the leading British and American German-to-English translation awards, and the German Federal Order of Merit for his writing and translation.

Adania Shibli has written novels, plays, short stories, and narrative essays. Her latest novel is *Tafsil Thanawi*, published in English as *Minor Detail* and a National Book Award finalist. Shibli is also a researcher in cultural studies and visual culture, and teaches part-time at Birzeit University, Palestine.

Stephen Snyder is Kawashima Professor of Japanese Studies at Middlebury College, where he serves as Vice President for Academic Affairs and Dean of Language Schools. He is the author of *Fictions of Desire: Narrative Form in the Novels of Nagai Kafū* and has translated works by Yoko Ogawa and Kenzaburo Oe, among other writers. His translation of Ogawa's *Memory Police* was a finalist for the National Book Award for Translated Literature and the International Booker Prize. He is currently working on a study of the publishing industry and its effect on literary canons in translation.

243

Christopher Stone is Associate Professor of Arabic at Hunter College of the City University of New York. He conducts research on Arab popular culture and is the author of *Popular Culture and Nationalism in Lebanon*. He has previously translated literary texts by Adania Shibli, Najwan Darwish, and Muin Bseiso for publication.

Mark Strand (1934–2014) was the author of many books of poems, a book of stories, and three volumes of translations, and was the editor of several anthologies. He received many honors and awards, including a MacArthur Fellowship, the Pulitzer Prize (for *Blizzard of One*), the Bollingen Prize, and the Gold Medal for Poetry from the American Academy of Arts and Letters. In 1990, he was appointed poet laureate of the United States.

Ginny Tapley Takemori has translated fiction by over a dozen early modern and contemporary Japanese authors. Her translation of Sayaka Murata's bestselling *Convenience Store Woman* was awarded the 2020–2021 Lindsley and Masao Miyoshi Prize. Her translation of Kyoko Nakajima's Naoki Prize–winning *The Little House* was published in 2019 and of Sayaka Murata's *Earthlings* in 2020. She lives in Japan.

Ocean Vuong is the author of *Night Sky with Exit Wounds* and *On Earth We're Briefly Gorgeous*. He was awarded a 2019 MacArthur Fellowship.

Alejandro Zambra was born in Santiago, Chile. The author of eight books including *Multiple Choice* and *My Documents*, his stories have been published in the *New Yorker*, *Harper's*, *Tin House*, and the *New York Times Magazine*, among others. The winner of numerous literary prizes, including an English PEN

Award and a Prince Claus Award (the Netherlands), he has also been a finalist for the Frank O'Connor International Short Story Award, the IMPAC Dublin Literary Award, and the Prix Médicis (France). He was named one of *Granta's* Best Young Spanish-Language Novelists in 2010. His new novel is forthcoming from Viking in 2022.

About the Editor

John Freeman was the editor of *Granta* until 2013. His books include *Dictionary of the Undoing, How to Read a Novelist, Tales of Two Americas*, and *Tales of Two Planets*. His poetry includes the collections *Maps, The Park,* and the forthcoming *Wind, Trees*. In 2021, he edited the anthologies *There's a Revolution Outside, My Love* with Tracy K.Smith, and *The Penguin Book of the Modern American Short Story*. An Executive Editor at Knopf, he teaches writing and literature classes at New York University. His work has appeared in the *New Yorker* and the *Paris Review* and has been translated into twenty-two languages.